C-1139  CAREER EXAMINATION SERIES

*This is your*
*PASSBOOK for...*

# Barber Instructor

*Test Preparation Study Guide*
*Questions & Answers*

NATIONAL LEARNING CORPORATION®

# COPYRIGHT NOTICE

This book is SOLELY intended for, is sold ONLY to, and its use is RESTRICTED to individual, bona fide applicants or candidates who qualify by virtue of having seriously filed applications for appropriate license, certificate, professional and/or promotional advancement, higher school matriculation, scholarship, or other legitimate requirements of education and/or governmental authorities.

This book is NOT intended for use, class instruction, tutoring, training, duplication, copying, reprinting, excerption, or adaptation, etc., by:

1) Other publishers
2) Proprietors and/or Instructors of "Coaching" and/or Preparatory Courses
3) Personnel and/or Training Divisions of commercial, industrial, and governmental organizations
4) Schools, colleges, or universities and/or their departments and staffs, including teachers and other personnel
5) Testing Agencies or Bureaus
6) Study groups which seek by the purchase of a single volume to copy and/or duplicate and/or adapt this material for use by the group as a whole without having purchased individual volumes for each of the members of the group
7) Et al.

Such persons would be in violation of appropriate Federal and State statutes.

PROVISION OF LICENSING AGREEMENTS – Recognized educational, commercial, industrial, and governmental institutions and organizations, and others legitimately engaged in educational pursuits, including training, testing, and measurement activities, may address request for a licensing agreement to the copyright owners, who will determine whether, and under what conditions, including fees and charges, the materials in this book may be used them.  In other words, a licensing facility exists for the legitimate use of the material in this book on other than an individual basis.  However, it is asseverated and affirmed here that the material in this book CANNOT be used without the receipt of the express permission of such a licensing agreement from the Publishers.  Inquiries re licensing should be addressed to the company, attention rights and permissions department.

All rights reserved, including the right of reproduction in whole or in part, in any form or by any means, electronic or mechanical, including photocopying, recording, or by any information storage and retrieval system, without permission in writing from the Publisher.

Copyright © 2024 by
## National Learning Corporation

212 Michael Drive, Syosset, NY 11791
(516) 921-8888 • www.passbooks.com
E-mail: info@passbooks.com

PUBLISHED IN THE UNITED STATES OF AMERICA

# PASSBOOK® SERIES

THE *PASSBOOK® SERIES* has been created to prepare applicants and candidates for the ultimate academic battlefield – the examination room.

At some time in our lives, each and every one of us may be required to take an examination – for validation, matriculation, admission, qualification, registration, certification, or licensure.

Based on the assumption that every applicant or candidate has met the basic formal educational standards, has taken the required number of courses, and read the necessary texts, the *PASSBOOK® SERIES* furnishes the one special preparation which may assure passing with confidence, instead of failing with insecurity. Examination questions – together with answers – are furnished as the basic vehicle for study so that the mysteries of the examination and its compounding difficulties may be eliminated or diminished by a sure method.

This book is meant to help you pass your examination provided that you qualify and are serious in your objective.

The entire field is reviewed through the huge store of content information which is succinctly presented through a provocative and challenging approach – the question-and-answer method.

A climate of success is established by furnishing the correct answers at the end of each test.

You soon learn to recognize types of questions, forms of questions, and patterns of questioning. You may even begin to anticipate expected outcomes.

You perceive that many questions are repeated or adapted so that you can gain acute insights, which may enable you to score many sure points.

You learn how to confront new questions, or types of questions, and to attack them confidently and work out the correct answers.

You note objectives and emphases, and recognize pitfalls and dangers, so that you may make positive educational adjustments.

Moreover, you are kept fully informed in relation to new concepts, methods, practices, and directions in the field.

You discover that you are actually taking the examination all the time: you are preparing for the examination by "taking" an examination, not by reading extraneous and/or supererogatory textbooks.

In short, this PASSBOOK®, used directedly, should be an important factor in helping you to pass your test.

# BARBER INSTRUCTOR

DUTIES

Barber instructors teach the responsibilities of barbering, such as shaving, cutting hair, styling hair, and performing chemical treatments to hair. The instructors also teach methods of achieving proper sanitation of barbershops that include individual, tool and equipment care. Barber's instructors are licensed professionals who teach the practice of barbering, hair cutting, and styling primarily for male clients, in private and vocational schools and community colleges. Instructors are typically experienced barbers, many of whom have received additional training through a certified instructor training program and acquired state licensure. The job entails preparing and teaching the material of a syllabus, mentoring and testing students, and grading students' work and exams. Barber's instructors may also be required to participate in school events and administrative meetings.

REQUISITES:
- A desire to develop teaching skills by attending training workshops.
- Demonstrate strong interpersonal and communication skills.
- Ensure excellent customer service and professionalism to all current and prospective students and co-workers at all times.
- Be a team player with a professional attitude.
- The desire to help to help others succeed in their career goals is required.
- Maintain a professional personal appearance and exercise good personal hygiene.
- Ability to provide a safe, positive, caring, and stimulating learning environment.

# HOW TO TAKE A TEST

I. YOU MUST PASS AN EXAMINATION

A. *WHAT EVERY CANDIDATE SHOULD KNOW*

Examination applicants often ask us for help in preparing for the written test. What can I study in advance? What kinds of questions will be asked? How will the test be given? How will the papers be graded?

As an applicant for a civil service examination, you may be wondering about some of these things. Our purpose here is to suggest effective methods of advance study and to describe civil service examinations.

Your chances for success on this examination can be increased if you know how to prepare. Those "pre-examination jitters" can be reduced if you know what to expect. You can even experience an adventure in good citizenship if you know why civil service exams are given.

B. *WHY ARE CIVIL SERVICE EXAMINATIONS GIVEN?*

Civil service examinations are important to you in two ways. As a citizen, you want public jobs filled by employees who know how to do their work. As a job seeker, you want a fair chance to compete for that job on an equal footing with other candidates. The best-known means of accomplishing this two-fold goal is the competitive examination.

Exams are widely publicized throughout the nation. They may be administered for jobs in federal, state, city, municipal, town or village governments or agencies.

Any citizen may apply, with some limitations, such as the age or residence of applicants. Your experience and education may be reviewed to see whether you meet the requirements for the particular examination. When these requirements exist, they are reasonable and applied consistently to all applicants. Thus, a competitive examination may cause you some uneasiness now, but it is your privilege and safeguard.

C. *HOW ARE CIVIL SERVICE EXAMS DEVELOPED?*

Examinations are carefully written by trained technicians who are specialists in the field known as "psychological measurement," in consultation with recognized authorities in the field of work that the test will cover. These experts recommend the subject matter areas or skills to be tested; only those knowledges or skills important to your success on the job are included. The most reliable books and source materials available are used as references. Together, the experts and technicians judge the difficulty level of the questions.

Test technicians know how to phrase questions so that the problem is clearly stated. Their ethics do not permit "trick" or "catch" questions. Questions may have been tried out on sample groups, or subjected to statistical analysis, to determine their usefulness.

Written tests are often used in combination with performance tests, ratings of training and experience, and oral interviews. All of these measures combine to form the best-known means of finding the right person for the right job.

## II. HOW TO PASS THE WRITTEN TEST

### A. NATURE OF THE EXAMINATION

To prepare intelligently for civil service examinations, you should know how they differ from school examinations you have taken. In school you were assigned certain definite pages to read or subjects to cover. The examination questions were quite detailed and usually emphasized memory. Civil service exams, on the other hand, try to discover your present ability to perform the duties of a position, plus your potentiality to learn these duties. In other words, a civil service exam attempts to predict how successful you will be. Questions cover such a broad area that they cannot be as minute and detailed as school exam questions.

In the public service similar kinds of work, or positions, are grouped together in one "class." This process is known as *position-classification*. All the positions in a class are paid according to the salary range for that class. One class title covers all of these positions, and they are all tested by the same examination.

### B. FOUR BASIC STEPS

#### 1) Study the announcement

How, then, can you know what subjects to study? Our best answer is: "Learn as much as possible about the class of positions for which you've applied." The exam will test the knowledge, skills and abilities needed to do the work.

Your most valuable source of information about the position you want is the official exam announcement. This announcement lists the training and experience qualifications. Check these standards and apply only if you come reasonably close to meeting them.

The brief description of the position in the examination announcement offers some clues to the subjects which will be tested. Think about the job itself. Review the duties in your mind. Can you perform them, or are there some in which you are rusty? Fill in the blank spots in your preparation.

Many jurisdictions preview the written test in the exam announcement by including a section called "Knowledge and Abilities Required," "Scope of the Examination," or some similar heading. Here you will find out specifically what fields will be tested.

#### 2) Review your own background

Once you learn in general what the position is all about, and what you need to know to do the work, ask yourself which subjects you already know fairly well and which need improvement. You may wonder whether to concentrate on improving your strong areas or on building some background in your fields of weakness. When the announcement has specified "some knowledge" or "considerable knowledge," or has used adjectives like "beginning principles of…" or "advanced … methods," you can get a clue as to the number and difficulty of questions to be asked in any given field. More questions, and hence broader coverage, would be included for those subjects which are more important in the work. Now weigh your strengths and weaknesses against the job requirements and prepare accordingly.

#### 3) Determine the level of the position

Another way to tell how intensively you should prepare is to understand the level of the job for which you are applying. Is it the entering level? In other words, is this the position in which beginners in a field of work are hired? Or is it an intermediate or advanced level? Sometimes this is indicated by such words as "Junior" or "Senior" in the class title. Other jurisdictions use Roman numerals to designate the level – Clerk I, Clerk II, for example. The word "Supervisor" sometimes appears in the title. If the level is not indicated by the title, check the description of duties. Will you be working under very close supervision, or will you have responsibility for independent decisions in this work?

### 4) Choose appropriate study materials

Now that you know the subjects to be examined and the relative amount of each subject to be covered, you can choose suitable study materials. For beginning level jobs, or even advanced ones, if you have a pronounced weakness in some aspect of your training, read a modern, standard textbook in that field. Be sure it is up to date and has general coverage. Such books are normally available at your library, and the librarian will be glad to help you locate one. For entry-level positions, questions of appropriate difficulty are chosen – neither highly advanced questions, nor those too simple. Such questions require careful thought but not advanced training.

If the position for which you are applying is technical or advanced, you will read more advanced, specialized material. If you are already familiar with the basic principles of your field, elementary textbooks would waste your time. Concentrate on advanced textbooks and technical periodicals. Think through the concepts and review difficult problems in your field.

These are all general sources. You can get more ideas on your own initiative, following these leads. For example, training manuals and publications of the government agency which employs workers in your field can be useful, particularly for technical and professional positions. A letter or visit to the government department involved may result in more specific study suggestions, and certainly will provide you with a more definite idea of the exact nature of the position you are seeking.

## III. KINDS OF TESTS

Tests are used for purposes other than measuring knowledge and ability to perform specified duties. For some positions, it is equally important to test ability to make adjustments to new situations or to profit from training. In others, basic mental abilities not dependent on information are essential. Questions which test these things may not appear as pertinent to the duties of the position as those which test for knowledge and information. Yet they are often highly important parts of a fair examination. For very general questions, it is almost impossible to help you direct your study efforts. What we can do is to point out some of the more common of these general abilities needed in public service positions and describe some typical questions.

### 1) General information

Broad, general information has been found useful for predicting job success in some kinds of work. This is tested in a variety of ways, from vocabulary lists to questions about current events. Basic background in some field of work, such as sociology or economics, may be sampled in a group of questions. Often these are principles which have become familiar to most persons through exposure rather than through formal training. It is difficult to advise you how to study for these questions; being alert to the world around you is our best suggestion.

### 2) Verbal ability

An example of an ability needed in many positions is verbal or language ability. Verbal ability is, in brief, the ability to use and understand words. Vocabulary and grammar tests are typical measures of this ability. Reading comprehension or paragraph interpretation questions are common in many kinds of civil service tests. You are given a paragraph of written material and asked to find its central meaning.

3) Numerical ability

Number skills can be tested by the familiar arithmetic problem, by checking paired lists of numbers to see which are alike and which are different, or by interpreting charts and graphs. In the latter test, a graph may be printed in the test booklet which you are asked to use as the basis for answering questions.

4) Observation

A popular test for law-enforcement positions is the observation test. A picture is shown to you for several minutes, then taken away. Questions about the picture test your ability to observe both details and larger elements.

5) Following directions

In many positions in the public service, the employee must be able to carry out written instructions dependably and accurately. You may be given a chart with several columns, each column listing a variety of information. The questions require you to carry out directions involving the information given in the chart.

6) Skills and aptitudes

Performance tests effectively measure some manual skills and aptitudes. When the skill is one in which you are trained, such as typing or shorthand, you can practice. These tests are often very much like those given in business school or high school courses. For many of the other skills and aptitudes, however, no short-time preparation can be made. Skills and abilities natural to you or that you have developed throughout your lifetime are being tested.

Many of the general questions just described provide all the data needed to answer the questions and ask you to use your reasoning ability to find the answers. Your best preparation for these tests, as well as for tests of facts and ideas, is to be at your physical and mental best. You, no doubt, have your own methods of getting into an exam-taking mood and keeping "in shape." The next section lists some ideas on this subject.

IV. KINDS OF QUESTIONS

Only rarely is the "essay" question, which you answer in narrative form, used in civil service tests. Civil service tests are usually of the short-answer type. Full instructions for answering these questions will be given to you at the examination. But in case this is your first experience with short-answer questions and separate answer sheets, here is what you need to know:

**1) Multiple-choice Questions**

Most popular of the short-answer questions is the "multiple choice" or "best answer" question. It can be used, for example, to test for factual knowledge, ability to solve problems or judgment in meeting situations found at work.

A multiple-choice question is normally one of three types—
- It can begin with an incomplete statement followed by several possible endings. You are to find the one ending which *best* completes the statement, although some of the others may not be entirely wrong.
- It can also be a complete statement in the form of a question which is answered by choosing one of the statements listed.

- It can be in the form of a problem – again you select the best answer.

Here is an example of a multiple-choice question with a discussion which should give you some clues as to the method for choosing the right answer:

When an employee has a complaint about his assignment, the action which will *best* help him overcome his difficulty is to
    A. discuss his difficulty with his coworkers
    B. take the problem to the head of the organization
    C. take the problem to the person who gave him the assignment
    D. say nothing to anyone about his complaint

In answering this question, you should study each of the choices to find which is best. Consider choice "A" – Certainly an employee may discuss his complaint with fellow employees, but no change or improvement can result, and the complaint remains unresolved. Choice "B" is a poor choice since the head of the organization probably does not know what assignment you have been given, and taking your problem to him is known as "going over the head" of the supervisor. The supervisor, or person who made the assignment, is the person who can clarify it or correct any injustice. Choice "C" is, therefore, correct. To say nothing, as in choice "D," is unwise. Supervisors have and interest in knowing the problems employees are facing, and the employee is seeking a solution to his problem.

## 2) True/False Questions

The "true/false" or "right/wrong" form of question is sometimes used. Here a complete statement is given. Your job is to decide whether the statement is right or wrong.

SAMPLE: A roaming cell-phone call to a nearby city costs less than a non-roaming call to a distant city.

This statement is wrong, or false, since roaming calls are more expensive.

This is not a complete list of all possible question forms, although most of the others are variations of these common types. You will always get complete directions for answering questions. Be sure you understand *how* to mark your answers – ask questions until you do.

## V. RECORDING YOUR ANSWERS

Computer terminals are used more and more today for many different kinds of exams.
For an examination with very few applicants, you may be told to record your answers in the test booklet itself. Separate answer sheets are much more common. If this separate answer sheet is to be scored by machine – and this is often the case – it is highly important that you mark your answers correctly in order to get credit.
An electronic scoring machine is often used in civil service offices because of the speed with which papers can be scored. Machine-scored answer sheets must be marked with a pencil, which will be given to you. This pencil has a high graphite content which responds to the electronic scoring machine. As a matter of fact, stray dots may register as answers, so do not let your pencil rest on the answer sheet while you are pondering the correct answer. Also, if your pencil lead breaks or is otherwise defective, ask for another.

Since the answer sheet will be dropped in a slot in the scoring machine, be careful not to bend the corners or get the paper crumpled.

The answer sheet normally has five vertical columns of numbers, with 30 numbers to a column. These numbers correspond to the question numbers in your test booklet. After each number, going across the page are four or five pairs of dotted lines. These short dotted lines have small letters or numbers above them. The first two pairs may also have a "T" or "F" above the letters. This indicates that the first two pairs only are to be used if the questions are of the true-false type. If the questions are multiple choice, disregard the "T" and "F" and pay attention only to the small letters or numbers.

Answer your questions in the manner of the sample that follows:

32. The largest city in the United States is
    A. Washington, D.C.
    B. New York City
    C. Chicago
    D. Detroit
    E. San Francisco

1) Choose the answer you think is best. (New York City is the largest, so "B" is correct.)
2) Find the row of dotted lines numbered the same as the question you are answering. (Find row number 32)
3) Find the pair of dotted lines corresponding to the answer. (Find the pair of lines under the mark "B.")
4) Make a solid black mark between the dotted lines.

## VI. BEFORE THE TEST

Common sense will help you find procedures to follow to get ready for an examination. Too many of us, however, overlook these sensible measures. Indeed, nervousness and fatigue have been found to be the most serious reasons why applicants fail to do their best on civil service tests. Here is a list of reminders:

- Begin your preparation early – Don't wait until the last minute to go scurrying around for books and materials or to find out what the position is all about.
- Prepare continuously – An hour a night for a week is better than an all-night cram session. This has been definitely established. What is more, a night a week for a month will return better dividends than crowding your study into a shorter period of time.
- Locate the place of the exam – You have been sent a notice telling you when and where to report for the examination. If the location is in a different town or otherwise unfamiliar to you, it would be well to inquire the best route and learn something about the building.
- Relax the night before the test – Allow your mind to rest. Do not study at all that night. Plan some mild recreation or diversion; then go to bed early and get a good night's sleep.
- Get up early enough to make a leisurely trip to the place for the test – This way unforeseen events, traffic snarls, unfamiliar buildings, etc. will not upset you.
- Dress comfortably – A written test is not a fashion show. You will be known by number and not by name, so wear something comfortable.

- Leave excess paraphernalia at home – Shopping bags and odd bundles will get in your way. You need bring only the items mentioned in the official notice you received; usually everything you need is provided. Do not bring reference books to the exam. They will only confuse those last minutes and be taken away from you when in the test room.
- Arrive somewhat ahead of time – If because of transportation schedules you must get there very early, bring a newspaper or magazine to take your mind off yourself while waiting.
- Locate the examination room – When you have found the proper room, you will be directed to the seat or part of the room where you will sit. Sometimes you are given a sheet of instructions to read while you are waiting. Do not fill out any forms until you are told to do so; just read them and be prepared.
- Relax and prepare to listen to the instructions
- If you have any physical problem that may keep you from doing your best, be sure to tell the test administrator. If you are sick or in poor health, you really cannot do your best on the exam. You can come back and take the test some other time.

## VII. AT THE TEST

The day of the test is here and you have the test booklet in your hand. The temptation to get going is very strong. Caution! There is more to success than knowing the right answers. You must know how to identify your papers and understand variations in the type of short-answer question used in this particular examination. Follow these suggestions for maximum results from your efforts:

### 1) Cooperate with the monitor

The test administrator has a duty to create a situation in which you can be as much at ease as possible. He will give instructions, tell you when to begin, check to see that you are marking your answer sheet correctly, and so on. He is not there to guard you, although he will see that your competitors do not take unfair advantage. He wants to help you do your best.

### 2) Listen to all instructions

Don't jump the gun! Wait until you understand all directions. In most civil service tests you get more time than you need to answer the questions. So don't be in a hurry. Read each word of instructions until you clearly understand the meaning. Study the examples, listen to all announcements and follow directions. Ask questions if you do not understand what to do.

### 3) Identify your papers

Civil service exams are usually identified by number only. You will be assigned a number; you must not put your name on your test papers. Be sure to copy your number correctly. Since more than one exam may be given, copy your exact examination title.

### 4) Plan your time

Unless you are told that a test is a "speed" or "rate of work" test, speed itself is usually not important. Time enough to answer all the questions will be provided, but this does not mean that you have all day. An overall time limit has been set. Divide the total time (in minutes) by the number of questions to determine the approximate time you have for each question.

### 5) Do not linger over difficult questions

If you come across a difficult question, mark it with a paper clip (useful to have along) and come back to it when you have been through the booklet. One caution if you do this – be sure to skip a number on your answer sheet as well. Check often to be sure that you have not lost your place and that you are marking in the row numbered the same as the question you are answering.

### 6) Read the questions

Be sure you know what the question asks! Many capable people are unsuccessful because they failed to *read* the questions correctly.

### 7) Answer all questions

Unless you have been instructed that a penalty will be deducted for incorrect answers, it is better to guess than to omit a question.

### 8) Speed tests

It is often better NOT to guess on speed tests. It has been found that on timed tests people are tempted to spend the last few seconds before time is called in marking answers at random – without even reading them – in the hope of picking up a few extra points. To discourage this practice, the instructions may warn you that your score will be "corrected" for guessing. That is, a penalty will be applied. The incorrect answers will be deducted from the correct ones, or some other penalty formula will be used.

### 9) Review your answers

If you finish before time is called, go back to the questions you guessed or omitted to give them further thought. Review other answers if you have time.

### 10) Return your test materials

If you are ready to leave before others have finished or time is called, take ALL your materials to the monitor and leave quietly. Never take any test material with you. The monitor can discover whose papers are not complete, and taking a test booklet may be grounds for disqualification.

## VIII. EXAMINATION TECHNIQUES

1) Read the general instructions carefully. These are usually printed on the first page of the exam booklet. As a rule, these instructions refer to the timing of the examination; the fact that you should not start work until the signal and must stop work at a signal, etc. If there are any *special* instructions, such as a choice of questions to be answered, make sure that you note this instruction carefully.

2) When you are ready to start work on the examination, that is as soon as the signal has been given, read the instructions to each question booklet, underline any key words or phrases, such as *least, best, outline, describe* and the like. In this way you will tend to answer as requested rather than discover on reviewing your paper that you *listed without describing*, that you selected the *worst* choice rather than the *best* choice, etc.

3) If the examination is of the objective or multiple-choice type – that is, each question will also give a series of possible answers: A, B, C or D, and you are called upon to select the best answer and write the letter next to that answer on your answer paper – it is advisable to start answering each question in turn. There may be anywhere from 50 to 100 such questions in the three or four hours allotted and you can see how much time would be taken if you read through all the questions before beginning to answer any. Furthermore, if you come across a question or group of questions which you know would be difficult to answer, it would undoubtedly affect your handling of all the other questions.

4) If the examination is of the essay type and contains but a few questions, it is a moot point as to whether you should read all the questions before starting to answer any one. Of course, if you are given a choice – say five out of seven and the like – then it is essential to read all the questions so you can eliminate the two that are most difficult. If, however, you are asked to answer all the questions, there may be danger in trying to answer the easiest one first because you may find that you will spend too much time on it. The best technique is to answer the first question, then proceed to the second, etc.

5) Time your answers. Before the exam begins, write down the time it started, then add the time allowed for the examination and write down the time it must be completed, then divide the time available somewhat as follows:
    - If 3-1/2 hours are allowed, that would be 210 minutes. If you have 80 objective-type questions, that would be an average of 2-1/2 minutes per question. Allow yourself no more than 2 minutes per question, or a total of 160 minutes, which will permit about 50 minutes to review.
    - If for the time allotment of 210 minutes there are 7 essay questions to answer, that would average about 30 minutes a question. Give yourself only 25 minutes per question so that you have about 35 minutes to review.

6) The most important instruction is to *read each question* and make sure you know what is wanted. The second most important instruction is to *time yourself properly* so that you answer every question. The third most important instruction is to *answer every question*. Guess if you have to but include something for each question. Remember that you will receive no credit for a blank and will probably receive some credit if you write something in answer to an essay question. If you guess a letter – say "B" for a multiple-choice question – you may have guessed right. If you leave a blank as an answer to a multiple-choice question, the examiners may respect your feelings but it will not add a point to your score. Some exams may penalize you for wrong answers, so in such cases *only*, you may not want to guess unless you have some basis for your answer.

7) Suggestions
    a. Objective-type questions
        1. Examine the question booklet for proper sequence of pages and questions
        2. Read all instructions carefully
        3. Skip any question which seems too difficult; return to it after all other questions have been answered
        4. Apportion your time properly; do not spend too much time on any single question or group of questions

5. Note and underline key words – *all, most, fewest, least, best, worst, same, opposite,* etc.
6. Pay particular attention to negatives
7. Note unusual option, e.g., unduly long, short, complex, different or similar in content to the body of the question
8. Observe the use of "hedging" words – *probably, may, most likely,* etc.
9. Make sure that your answer is put next to the same number as the question
10. Do not second-guess unless you have good reason to believe the second answer is definitely more correct
11. Cross out original answer if you decide another answer is more accurate; do not erase until you are ready to hand your paper in
12. Answer all questions; guess unless instructed otherwise
13. Leave time for review

   b. Essay questions
     1. Read each question carefully
     2. Determine exactly what is wanted. Underline key words or phrases.
     3. Decide on outline or paragraph answer
     4. Include many different points and elements unless asked to develop any one or two points or elements
     5. Show impartiality by giving pros and cons unless directed to select one side only
     6. Make and write down any assumptions you find necessary to answer the questions
     7. Watch your English, grammar, punctuation and choice of words
     8. Time your answers; don't crowd material

8) Answering the essay question

Most essay questions can be answered by framing the specific response around several key words or ideas. Here are a few such key words or ideas:

M's: manpower, materials, methods, money, management
P's: purpose, program, policy, plan, procedure, practice, problems, pitfalls, personnel, public relations

   a. Six basic steps in handling problems:
     1. Preliminary plan and background development
     2. Collect information, data and facts
     3. Analyze and interpret information, data and facts
     4. Analyze and develop solutions as well as make recommendations
     5. Prepare report and sell recommendations
     6. Install recommendations and follow up effectiveness

   b. Pitfalls to avoid
     1. *Taking things for granted* – A statement of the situation does not necessarily imply that each of the elements is necessarily true; for example, a complaint may be invalid and biased so that all that can be taken for granted is that a complaint has been registered

2. *Considering only one side of a situation* – Wherever possible, indicate several alternatives and then point out the reasons you selected the best one
3. *Failing to indicate follow up* – Whenever your answer indicates action on your part, make certain that you will take proper follow-up action to see how successful your recommendations, procedures or actions turn out to be
4. *Taking too long in answering any single question* – Remember to time your answers properly

## IX. AFTER THE TEST

Scoring procedures differ in detail among civil service jurisdictions although the general principles are the same. Whether the papers are hand-scored or graded by machine we have described, they are nearly always graded by number. That is, the person who marks the paper knows only the number – never the name – of the applicant. Not until all the papers have been graded will they be matched with names. If other tests, such as training and experience or oral interview ratings have been given, scores will be combined. Different parts of the examination usually have different weights. For example, the written test might count 60 percent of the final grade, and a rating of training and experience 40 percent. In many jurisdictions, veterans will have a certain number of points added to their grades.

After the final grade has been determined, the names are placed in grade order and an eligible list is established. There are various methods for resolving ties between those who get the same final grade – probably the most common is to place first the name of the person whose application was received first. Job offers are made from the eligible list in the order the names appear on it. You will be notified of your grade and your rank as soon as all these computations have been made. This will be done as rapidly as possible.

People who are found to meet the requirements in the announcement are called "eligibles." Their names are put on a list of eligible candidates. An eligible's chances of getting a job depend on how high he stands on this list and how fast agencies are filling jobs from the list.

When a job is to be filled from a list of eligibles, the agency asks for the names of people on the list of eligibles for that job. When the civil service commission receives this request, it sends to the agency the names of the three people highest on this list. Or, if the job to be filled has specialized requirements, the office sends the agency the names of the top three persons who meet these requirements from the general list.

The appointing officer makes a choice from among the three people whose names were sent to him. If the selected person accepts the appointment, the names of the others are put back on the list to be considered for future openings.

That is the rule in hiring from all kinds of eligible lists, whether they are for typist, carpenter, chemist, or something else. For every vacancy, the appointing officer has his choice of any one of the top three eligibles on the list. This explains why the person whose name is on top of the list sometimes does not get an appointment when some of the persons lower on the list do. If the appointing officer chooses the second or third eligible, the No. 1 eligible does not get a job at once, but stays on the list until he is appointed or the list is terminated.

# X. HOW TO PASS THE INTERVIEW TEST

The examination for which you applied requires an oral interview test. You have already taken the written test and you are now being called for the interview test – the final part of the formal examination.

You may think that it is not possible to prepare for an interview test and that there are no procedures to follow during an interview. Our purpose is to point out some things you can do in advance that will help you and some good rules to follow and pitfalls to avoid while you are being interviewed.

*What is an interview supposed to test?*

The written examination is designed to test the technical knowledge and competence of the candidate; the oral is designed to evaluate intangible qualities, not readily measured otherwise, and to establish a list showing the relative fitness of each candidate – as measured against his competitors – for the position sought. Scoring is not on the basis of "right" and "wrong," but on a sliding scale of values ranging from "not passable" to "outstanding." As a matter of fact, it is possible to achieve a relatively low score without a single "incorrect" answer because of evident weakness in the qualities being measured.

Occasionally, an examination may consist entirely of an oral test – either an individual or a group oral. In such cases, information is sought concerning the technical knowledges and abilities of the candidate, since there has been no written examination for this purpose. More commonly, however, an oral test is used to supplement a written examination.

*Who conducts interviews?*

The composition of oral boards varies among different jurisdictions. In nearly all, a representative of the personnel department serves as chairman. One of the members of the board may be a representative of the department in which the candidate would work. In some cases, "outside experts" are used, and, frequently, a businessman or some other representative of the general public is asked to serve. Labor and management or other special groups may be represented. The aim is to secure the services of experts in the appropriate field.

However the board is composed, it is a good idea (and not at all improper or unethical) to ascertain in advance of the interview who the members are and what groups they represent. When you are introduced to them, you will have some idea of their backgrounds and interests, and at least you will not stutter and stammer over their names.

*What should be done before the interview?*

While knowledge about the board members is useful and takes some of the surprise element out of the interview, there is other preparation which is more substantive. It *is* possible to prepare for an oral interview – in several ways:

**1) Keep a copy of your application and review it carefully before the interview**

This may be the only document before the oral board, and the starting point of the interview. Know what education and experience you have listed there, and the sequence and dates of all of it. Sometimes the board will ask you to review the highlights of your experience for them; you should not have to hem and haw doing it.

**2) Study the class specification and the examination announcement**

Usually, the oral board has one or both of these to guide them. The qualities, characteristics or knowledges required by the position sought are stated in these documents. They offer valuable clues as to the nature of the oral interview. For example, if the job involves supervisory responsibilities, the announcement will usually indicate that knowledge of modern supervisory methods and the qualifications of the candidate as a supervisor will be tested. If so, you can expect such questions, frequently in the form of a hypothetical situation which you are expected to solve. NEVER go into an oral without knowledge of the duties and responsibilities of the job you seek.

### 3) Think through each qualification required

Try to visualize the kind of questions you would ask if you were a board member. How well could you answer them? Try especially to appraise your own knowledge and background in each area, *measured against the job sought*, and identify any areas in which you are weak. Be critical and realistic – do not flatter yourself.

### 4) Do some general reading in areas in which you feel you may be weak

For example, if the job involves supervision and your past experience has NOT, some general reading in supervisory methods and practices, particularly in the field of human relations, might be useful. Do NOT study agency procedures or detailed manuals. The oral board will be testing your understanding and capacity, not your memory.

### 5) Get a good night's sleep and watch your general health and mental attitude

You will want a clear head at the interview. Take care of a cold or any other minor ailment, and of course, no hangovers.

*What should be done on the day of the interview?*

Now comes the day of the interview itself. Give yourself plenty of time to get there. Plan to arrive somewhat ahead of the scheduled time, particularly if your appointment is in the fore part of the day. If a previous candidate fails to appear, the board might be ready for you a bit early. By early afternoon an oral board is almost invariably behind schedule if there are many candidates, and you may have to wait. Take along a book or magazine to read, or your application to review, but leave any extraneous material in the waiting room when you go in for your interview. In any event, relax and compose yourself.

The matter of dress is important. The board is forming impressions about you – from your experience, your manners, your attitude, and your appearance. Give your personal appearance careful attention. Dress your best, but not your flashiest. Choose conservative, appropriate clothing, and be sure it is immaculate. This is a business interview, and your appearance should indicate that you regard it as such. Besides, being well groomed and properly dressed will help boost your confidence.

Sooner or later, someone will call your name and escort you into the interview room. *This is it.* From here on you are on your own. It is too late for any more preparation. But remember, you asked for this opportunity to prove your fitness, and you are here because your request was granted.

*What happens when you go in?*

The usual sequence of events will be as follows: The clerk (who is often the board stenographer) will introduce you to the chairman of the oral board, who will introduce you to the other members of the board. Acknowledge the introductions before you sit down. Do not be surprised if you find a microphone facing you or a stenotypist sitting by. Oral interviews are usually recorded in the event of an appeal or other review.

Usually the chairman of the board will open the interview by reviewing the highlights of your education and work experience from your application – primarily for the benefit of the other members of the board, as well as to get the material into the record. Do not interrupt or comment unless there is an error or significant misinterpretation; if that is the case, do not hesitate. But do not quibble about insignificant matters. Also, he will usually ask you some question about your education, experience or your present job – partly to get you to start talking and to establish the interviewing "rapport." He may start the actual questioning, or turn it over to one of the other members. Frequently, each member undertakes the questioning on a particular area, one in which he is perhaps most competent, so you can expect each member to participate in the examination. Because time is limited, you may also expect some rather abrupt switches in the direction the questioning takes, so do not be upset by it. Normally, a board member will not pursue a single line of questioning unless he discovers a particular strength or weakness.

After each member has participated, the chairman will usually ask whether any member has any further questions, then will ask you if you have anything you wish to add. Unless you are expecting this question, it may floor you. Worse, it may start you off on an extended, extemporaneous speech. The board is not usually seeking more information. The question is principally to offer you a last opportunity to present further qualifications or to indicate that you have nothing to add. So, if you feel that a significant qualification or characteristic has been overlooked, it is proper to point it out in a sentence or so. Do not compliment the board on the thoroughness of their examination -- they have been sketchy, and you know it. If you wish, merely say, "No thank you, I have nothing further to add." This is a point where you can "talk yourself out" of a good impression or fail to present an important bit of information. Remember, *you close the interview yourself*.

The chairman will then say, "That is all, Mr. _____, thank you." Do not be startled; the interview is over, and quicker than you think. Thank him, gather your belongings and take your leave. Save your sigh of relief for the other side of the door.

*How to put your best foot forward*

Throughout this entire process, you may feel that the board individually and collectively is trying to pierce your defenses, seek out your hidden weaknesses and embarrass and confuse you. Actually, this is not true. They are obliged to make an appraisal of your qualifications for the job you are seeking, and they want to see you in your best light. Remember, they must interview all candidates and a non-cooperative candidate may become a failure in spite of their best efforts to bring out his qualifications. Here are 15 suggestions that will help you:

**1) Be natural – Keep your attitude confident, not cocky**

If you are not confident that you can do the job, do not expect the board to be. Do not apologize for your weaknesses, try to bring out your strong points. The board is interested in a positive, not negative, presentation. Cockiness will antagonize any board member and make him wonder if you are covering up a weakness by a false show of strength.

**2) Get comfortable, but don't lounge or sprawl**

Sit erectly but not stiffly. A careless posture may lead the board to conclude that you are careless in other things, or at least that you are not impressed by the importance of the occasion. Either conclusion is natural, even if incorrect. Do not fuss with your clothing, a pencil or an ashtray. Your hands may occasionally be useful to emphasize a point; do not let them become a point of distraction.

**3) Do not wisecrack or make small talk**

This is a serious situation, and your attitude should show that you consider it as such. Further, the time of the board is limited – they do not want to waste it, and neither should you.

### 4) Do not exaggerate your experience or abilities
In the first place, from information in the application or other interviews and sources, the board may know more about you than you think. Secondly, you probably will not get away with it. An experienced board is rather adept at spotting such a situation, so do not take the chance.

### 5) If you know a board member, do not make a point of it, yet do not hide it
Certainly you are not fooling him, and probably not the other members of the board. Do not try to take advantage of your acquaintanceship – it will probably do you little good.

### 6) Do not dominate the interview
Let the board do that. They will give you the clues – do not assume that you have to do all the talking. Realize that the board has a number of questions to ask you, and do not try to take up all the interview time by showing off your extensive knowledge of the answer to the first one.

### 7) Be attentive
You only have 20 minutes or so, and you should keep your attention at its sharpest throughout. When a member is addressing a problem or question to you, give him your undivided attention. Address your reply principally to him, but do not exclude the other board members.

### 8) Do not interrupt
A board member may be stating a problem for you to analyze. He will ask you a question when the time comes. Let him state the problem, and wait for the question.

### 9) Make sure you understand the question
Do not try to answer until you are sure what the question is. If it is not clear, restate it in your own words or ask the board member to clarify it for you. However, do not haggle about minor elements.

### 10) Reply promptly but not hastily
A common entry on oral board rating sheets is "candidate responded readily," or "candidate hesitated in replies." Respond as promptly and quickly as you can, but do not jump to a hasty, ill-considered answer.

### 11) Do not be peremptory in your answers
A brief answer is proper – but do not fire your answer back. That is a losing game from your point of view. The board member can probably ask questions much faster than you can answer them.

### 12) Do not try to create the answer you think the board member wants
He is interested in what kind of mind you have and how it works – not in playing games. Furthermore, he can usually spot this practice and will actually grade you down on it.

### 13) Do not switch sides in your reply merely to agree with a board member
Frequently, a member will take a contrary position merely to draw you out and to see if you are willing and able to defend your point of view. Do not start a debate, yet do not surrender a good position. If a position is worth taking, it is worth defending.

**14) Do not be afraid to admit an error in judgment if you are shown to be wrong**

The board knows that you are forced to reply without any opportunity for careful consideration. Your answer may be demonstrably wrong. If so, admit it and get on with the interview.

**15) Do not dwell at length on your present job**

The opening question may relate to your present assignment. Answer the question but do not go into an extended discussion. You are being examined for a *new* job, not your present one. As a matter of fact, try to phrase ALL your answers in terms of the job for which you are being examined.

*Basis of Rating*

Probably you will forget most of these "do's" and "don'ts" when you walk into the oral interview room. Even remembering them all will not ensure you a passing grade. Perhaps you did not have the qualifications in the first place. But remembering them will help you to put your best foot forward, without treading on the toes of the board members.

Rumor and popular opinion to the contrary notwithstanding, an oral board wants you to make the best appearance possible. They know you are under pressure – but they also want to see how you respond to it as a guide to what your reaction would be under the pressures of the job you seek. They will be influenced by the degree of poise you display, the personal traits you show and the manner in which you respond.

ABOUT THIS BOOK

This book contains tests divided into Examination Sections. Go through each test, answering every question in the margin. We have also attached a sample answer sheet at the back of the book that can be removed and used. At the end of each test look at the answer key and check your answers. On the ones you got wrong, look at the right answer choice and learn. Do not fill in the answers first. Do not memorize the questions and answers, but understand the answer and principles involved. On your test, the questions will likely be different from the samples. Questions are changed and new ones added. If you understand these past questions you should have success with any changes that arise. Tests may consist of several types of questions. We have additional books on each subject should more study be advisable or necessary for you. Finally, the more you study, the better prepared you will be. This book is intended to be the last thing you study before you walk into the examination room. Prior study of relevant texts is also recommended. NLC publishes some of these in our Fundamental Series. Knowledge and good sense are important factors in passing your exam. Good luck also helps. So now study this Passbook, absorb the material contained within and take that knowledge into the examination. Then do your best to pass that exam.

# EXAMINATION SECTION

# EXAMINATION SECTION
# TEST 1

DIRECTIONS: Each question or incomplete statement is followed by several suggested answers or completions. Select the one that best answers the question or completes the statement. *PRINT THE LETTER OF THE CORRECT ANSWER IN THE SPACE AT THE RIGHT.*

1. To enhance a student's acceptance of further instruction, the instructor should     1.____

    A. emphasize the student's inabilities
    B. keep the student informed of the progress made
    C. establish performance standards a little above the student's actual ability
    D. inform the student that others in the class are progressing faster

2. The basis on which evaluation of student performance and accomplishment should be made is established during which step in the teaching process?     2.____

    A. Presentation
    B. Preparation
    C. Application
    D. Review and evaluation

3. Before the end of each instructional period, the instructor should     3.____

    A. conduct a subjective evaluation of the student's performance
    B. emphasize that mastery of the task is more important than complete understanding
    C. introduce the main features and objectives of the next lesson
    D. require the student to demonstrate the extent to which the lesson objectives have been met

4. Evaluation of student performance and accomplishment during a lesson should be based on the     4.____

    A. student's actual performance as compared to a faultless performance
    B. student's background and past experiences
    C. direct comparison with the performance of other students in the class
    D. objectives and goals that were established in the lesson plan

5. Which statement is TRUE regarding student evaluation?     5.____

    A. Evaluation of a student's learning should be an integral part of each classroom lesson.
    B. The preferred method of quizzing a student is by asking questions which can be answered by a *yes* or a *no*.
    C. Tests should be developed in such a manner that no one can get a perfect score.
    D. Ambiguous questions tend to force one to think therefore, they are acceptable when evaluating students.

6. Suppose during a review and evaluation of things previously learned, a deficiency or fault exists in the knowledge or performances on which the present lesson is predicated. What should the instructor do?     6.____

    A. Correct the deficiency or fault before a new lesson is begun.
    B. Repeat the present lesson until the deficiency is corrected.

C. Carefully note and point out the deficiency or fault and go on to the next new lesson.
D. Include remedial actions in the next new lesson.

7. At the beginning of the student's lesson, during early instruction, the instructor should

   A. avoid terms and phrases which are part of the new topic since they are new and strange to the student
   B. define the terms and phrases which will be used during the forthcoming lesson
   C. use colloquial expressions so the student can learn the language
   D. use picturesque expressions to brighten the instruction given

8. Which statement is TRUE regarding positive or negative approaches in instructional techniques?

   A. A negative teaching approach generally results in positive learning.
   B. Negative approaches are more effective than positive approaches.
   C. Positive approaches point out the pleasurable features before the critical possibilities are stressed.
   D. To be effective, instructors should ignore the existence of negative factors.

9. Which statement is TRUE regarding positive or negative approaches in instruction?

   A. Negative approaches are generally more effective than positive approaches.
   B. A positive approach is one which stresses all the critical possibilities before the potential and pleasurable features are presented.
   C. The positive approach of introducing new procedures after the student is acquainted with normal procedures is not likely to be discouraging or frightening for the student.
   D. A positive approach will stress that a procedure must be accomplished in a certain manner or serious consequences will result.

10. Which of these is an example of a positive approach in the first lesson of a student with no previous experience?

    A. Instruction must be vague for fear course may prove difficult.
    B. A series of inconsequential data is used.
    C. A series of review of previous term's work is introduced.
    D. Introducing the subject slowly and concisely.

11. The _____ method of presentation is desirable for a lesson on a skill such as the use of a computer.

    A. demonstration/performance    B. informal lecture
    C. formal lecture               D. guided discussion

12. In the teaching process, the _____ method of presentation is suitable for presenting new material, for summarizing ideas, and for showing relationships between theory and practice.

    A. demonstration/performance    B. guided discussion
    C. lecture                      D. integrated instruction

13. The linear-programmed instruction method is based *primarily* on  13.____

    A. referral to previously learned subjects
    B. punishment for incorrect responses
    C. involvement in class discussions
    D. reinforcement (reward) for accurate performance

14. Students should perform an operation the right way the first few times because  14.____

    A. it establishes the basis for evaluation of the students' overall performance
    B. that is when habits are established
    C. it allows an earlier introduction of a new lesson
    D. it requires less supervision and coaching by the instructor

15. What is the PROPER sequence in which the instructor should employ the four basic steps in the teaching process?  15.____

    A. Explanation, trial and practice, evaluation, and review
    B. Explanation, demonstration, practice, and evaluation
    C. Presentation, trial and practice, evaluation, and review
    D. Preparation, presentation, application, and review and evaluation

16. An instructor who uses the student's previous experiences and knowledge as a starting point and leads into new ideas and concepts is teaching from the  16.____

    A. least frequently used to most frequently used
    B. simple to complex
    C. known to the unknown
    D. most frequently used to least frequently used

17. The method of arranging lesson material from the simple to complex, past to present, and known to unknown, is one that  17.____

    A. the instructor should avoid
    B. creates student thought pattern departures
    C. covers the areas only briefly in a normal discussion
    D. shows the relationships of the main points of the lesson

18. When teaching from the *known* to the *unknown*, an instructor is using the student's  18.____

    A. negative self-concepts
    B. anxieties and insecurities
    C. previous experiences and knowledge
    D. likes and dislikes

19. In organizing lesson material, which step should relate the coverage of material to the entire course?  19.____

    A. Conclusion         B. Overview
    C. Development        D. Introduction

20. In developing a lesson, the instructor must logically : organize explanations and demonstrations to help the student

    A. learn by trial-and-error practice of the procedures
    B. understand the relationships of the main points of the lesson
    C. experience a minimum amount of difficulty in memorizing the steps of a procedure
    D. learn by rote so that performance of the procedure will become automatic

21. Should an instructor be concerned about an apt student who makes very few mistakes?

    A. *Yes;* the student will lose confidence in the instructor unless the instructor invents deficiencies in the student's performance
    B. *No;* this is an indication that the student will perform flawlessly.
    C. *No;* the correction of such a student's mistakes is unimportant and unnecessary.
    D. *Yes;* faulty performance may soon appear due to student overconfidence.

22. What should an instructor do if a student is suspected of not fully understanding the principles involved in a task, even though the student can correctly perform the task?

    A. Require the student to apply the same elements to the performance of other tasks.
    B. Emphasize that mastery of the task is more important than complete understanding.
    C. Introduce a more complicated task and ask the student to explain the elements involved.
    D. Construct a specific and factual oral or written quiz which requires a simple *yes* or *no* answer.

23. When reviewing the lesson, the instructor should recapitulate what has been covered during the lesson to

    A. improve the student's grades, based upon the objectives and goals of the lesson plan and syllabus
    B. ensure that the student is aware of the progress made
    C. emphasize the competitive nature of the learning situation
    D. identify the blocks of learning which constitute the necessary parts of the total objective

24. Which of these should be omitted from an instructor's critique of a student's performance?

    A. Instruction in the form of direction and guidance
    B. Negative criticism that does not point toward improvement
    C. The student's strengths and successes
    D. The student's personal feelings

25. Which statement is TRUE about an instructor's critique of a student's performance?

    A. The student's personal feelings should not enter into the critique.
    B. It should be constructive and objective.
    C. It should treat every aspect of the performance in detail.
    D. By its nature, a critique is necessarily negative in content.

# KEY (CORRECT ANSWERS)

| | | | |
|---|---|---|---|
| 1. | B | 11. | D |
| 2. | D | 12. | D |
| 3. | D | 13. | D |
| 4. | D | 14. | B |
| 5. | A | 15. | D |
| 6. | A | 16. | C |
| 7. | B | 17. | D |
| 8. | C | 18. | C |
| 9. | C | 19. | B |
| 10. | D | 20. | B |

21. D
22. A
23. D
24. B
25. B

# TEST 2

DIRECTIONS: Each question or incomplete statement is followed by several suggested answers or completions. Select the one that BEST answers the question or completes the statement. *PRINT THE LETTER OF THE CORRECT ANSWER IN THE SPACE AT THE RIGHT.*

1. Which statement is TRUE about instructors' critiques?　　　　　　　　　　　　　　　　1.___

    A. Instructors should rely on their position to make a critique more acceptable to their students.
    B. Before students willingly accept their instructors' critique, they must first accept the instructor.
    C. Critiques must be inflexible and not allow for variables.
    D. A comprehensive critique must treat every aspect of the student's performance in detail.

2. The purpose of a critique of the student's performance is to　　　　　　　　　　　　　2.___

    A. instill student confidence in the instructor's ability and authority
    B. provide direction and guidance to raise the level of the student's performance
    C. identify only the student's faults and weaknesses
    D. evaluate the student and assign a grade

3. Which statement is TRUE about an instructor's critique of a student's performance?　　3.___

    A. The critique should be subjective rather than objective in nature.
    B. It is a step in the learning process, not in the grading process.
    C. By its nature, a critique is necessarily negative in content.
    D. The instructor's comments and recommendations should be general rather than specific.

4. An instructor's critique of a student's performance should　　　　　　　　　　　　　　4.___

    A. treat every aspect of the performance in detail
    B. identify only the faults and weaknesses
    C. clearly express what was done well, what was done poorly, and how to improve the performance
    D. be conducted only in private

5. When an instructor critiques a student, it should ALWAYS be　　　　　　　　　　　　5.___

    A. conducted immediately after the student's performance
    B. subjective rather than objective
    C. done in private
    D. designed and executed so that the instructor cannot allow for variables

6. When conducting a critique, the instructor should　　　　　　　　　　　　　　　　　　6.___

    A. cover only a few well-made points rather than a large number of inadequately developed points
    B. cover all of the student's faults or weaknesses, large and small
    C. emphasize the points covered with dogmatic and absolute statements
    D. praise the student before criticizing, even if undeserved

7. When conducting a critique, the instructor should 7._____

    A. cover all of the student's faults or weaknesses, large and small
    B. avoid trying to cover too much material
    C. emphasize the points covered with dogmatic and absolute statements
    D. praise the student before criticizing, even if undeserved

8. Of the following, which is a VALID reason for the use of proper oral quizzing during a lesson? It 8._____

    A. permits the instructor to devote more time to helping weak students rather than developing written tests
    B. helps the instructor determine the general intelligence level of the students
    C. promotes active student participation
    D. is unnecessary to grade the results

9. To be effective in oral quizzing during the conduct of a lesson, a question should 9._____

    A. divert the student's thoughts to subjects covered in other lessons
    B. center on only one idea
    C. be easy for the student at that particular stage of training
    D. include a combination of where, how, and why

10. During oral quizzing in a given lesson, effective questions should 10._____

    A. divert the student's thoughts to subjects covered in previous lessons
    B. relate to more than one thought or idea
    C. include a combination of who, what, when, or where
    D. be difficult for the student at that particular stage of training

11. To answer a student's question, it is MOST important that the instructor 11._____

    A. clearly understand the qxiestion
    B. risk a guess rather than admit ignorance
    C. keep specifics to a minimum
    D. have complete knowledge of the subject

12. If a student asks a question which the instructor CANNOT answer, the instructor should 12._____

    A. tell the student to reintroduce the question later, to allow time for the instructor to research the answer
    B. inform the student the question is irrelevant and not pertinent to the subject being covered
    C. admit not knowing the answer and promise to get the answer or help find the answer
    D. tell the student to find the answer in available references

13. One desirable result of proper oral quizzing by the instructor is to 13._____

    A. establish a grade for the student
    B. reveal the effectiveness of the instructor's training procedures
    C. fulfill the requirements set forth in the overall objectives of the course
    D. reveal the essential information from which the student can determine progress

14. Proper quizzing by the instructor during a lesson can have which of these results?  14.___

    A. It diverts the student's thoughts to unrelated subjects
    B. It permits the introduction of new material which was not covered previously.
    C. It identifies points which need more emphasis.
    D. It develops a feeling in the student of matching wits with the instructor.

15. In all quizzing as a portion of the instruction process, the questions should  15.___

    A. include catch questions to develop the student's perceptive power
    B. include unrelated subject matter to increase total comprehension
    C. include questions with more than one central idea to evaluate how completely a student understands the subject
    D. call for specific answers and be readily evaluated by the instructor

16. One of the MAIN advantages of selection-type (multiple choice) test items over supply-types (essay) test items is that the selection-type  16.___

    A. precludes comparison of students under one instructor with those under another instructor
    B. requires students to organize their knowledge
    C. would be graded objectively regardless of the student or the grader
    D. demands the ability of students to express ideas

17. Which statement is TRUE relative to effective multiple-choice type test items?  17.___

    A. Students should be able to select the correct response only if they know it is correct.
    B. It is not ethical to mislead the unknowledgeable student into selecting an incorrect alternative.
    C. Common errors or misconceptions should not be used as incorrect alternatives.
    D. Students should be able to select the correct response with even slight knowledge of the subject.

18. Which statement is TRUE about multiple-choice type test items that are intended to measure achievement at a higher level of learning?  18.___

    A. If there are less than four alternatives, the probability of guessing the correct response is decreased.
    B. It is unethical to mislead the unknowledgeable student into selecting an incorrect alternative.
    C. The use of common errors as distracting alternatives to divert the student from the correct response is ineffective and invalid.
    D. Some or all of the alternatives should be nearly correct but only one should be clearly correct.

19. In developing multiple-choice type test items and the alternative responses, it is  19.___

    A. proper to include as an alternative response a statement which itself is true but does not satisfy the requirements of the problem
    B. ineffective and invalid to use common errors as distracting alternatives
    C. more likely the test will contain ambiguities but will give more clues to the correct response
    D. ethical to mislead the unknowledgeable student into selecting an incorrect alternative

20. In a written test, the _____ type of test items makes it easier to compare the performance of students within the same class or in different classes.

    A. selection
    B. true-false
    C. essay
    D. supply

21. One of the MAJOR difficulties encountered in the construction of multiple-choice type test items is

    A. inventing distractors which will be attractive to students lacking knowledge or understanding
    B. phrasing the item in question form in lieu of statement form
    C. adapting the items to statistical item analysis
    D. keeping all responses approximately equal in length

22. The _____ type of test item creates the GREATEST probability of guessing.

    A. multiple-choice
    B. true-false
    C. selection
    D. supply

23. Which of the following principles should be followed in the development of true-false type tests?

    A. Include complex statements in the questions
    B. Include one or more ideas in each statement in the questions
    C. Avoid absolutes such as *all, every,* and *only*
    D. Establish patterns in the sequence of correct responses for easier scoring

24. A characteristic of supply-type (essay) test items is the

    A. ability of the student to express ideas is not required
    B. student's specific knowledge of subject matter is readily evaluated
    C. test results would be graded the same regardless of the student or the grader
    D. same test graded by different instructors would probably be given different scores

25. Which of the following is the MAIN disadvantage of supply-type (essay) test items? They

    A. increase the probability of student guessing
    B. make it possible to directly compare student accomplishment
    C. do not require students to organize their knowledge
    D. cannot be graded with uniformity

## KEY (CORRECT ANSWERS)

1. B
2. B
3. B
4. C
5. A

6. A
7. B
8. C
9. B
10. D

11. A
12. C
13. B
14. C
15. D

16. C
17. A
18. D
19. A
20. A

21. A
22. B
23. C
24. D
25. D

# TEST 3

DIRECTIONS: Each question or incomplete statement is followed by several suggested answers or completions. Select the one that BEST answers the question or completes the statement. *PRINT THE LETTER OF THE CORRECT ANSWER IN TE SPACE AT THE RIGHT.*

1. The characteristic of a written test which measures small differences in achievement between students is its

   A. validity
   B. comprehensiveness
   C. discrimination
   D. reliability

   1.____

2. When a written test shows positive discrimination, it will

   A. distinguish between the students who are low and those who are high in achievement
   B. sample liberally what is being measured
   C. not measure what is intended
   D. include a representative and comprehensive sampling of the course objectives

   2.____

3. A written test is said to be *comprehensive* when it

   A. includes all levels of difficulty
   B. measures knowledge of the same topic in many different ways
   C. samples liberally whatever is being measured
   D. shows a wide range of scores

   3.____

4. A written test has *validity* when it

   A. measures small differences in the achievement of students
   B. samples liberally whatever is being measured
   C. yields consistent results
   D. actually measures what it is supposed to measure and nothing else

   4.____

5. A written test which has *reliability* is one which

   A. yields consistent results
   B. samples liberally whatever is being measured
   C. measures small differences in the achievement of students
   D. actually measures what it is supposed to measure and nothing else

   5.____

6. Development and assembly of *blocks of learning* in their proper relationship will provide a means for

   A. allowing the student to master the segments of the overall performance requirements individually and combining these with other related segments
   B. taking full advantage of both positive and negative transfer of learning
   C. eliminating the need to master initial instruction in the simple elements of a task before more advanced operations can be introduced
   D. both the instructor and student to easily correct faulty habit patterns

   6.____

11

7. Which statement is TRUE regarding course syllabi? They should be

   A. followed rigidly if maximum benefit is to be derived from their use
   B. altered to suit the student's progress and the demands of special circumstances
   C. used primarily by inexperienced instructors
   D. used primarily when teaching students who have already received part of their training from another instructor

8. When it is impossible to conduct a scheduled lesson, it is preferable for the instructor to

   A. revise the lesson objective
   B. conduct a lesson that is not predicated completely on skills to be developed during the lesson which was postponed
   C. proceed to the next scheduled lesson, or if this is not practical, cancel the lesson
   D. postpone all lessons until the scheduled lesson can be completed

9. Which of the following statements is TRUE concerning extraneous blocks of instruction during a course of training?
   They

   A. assist in the attainment of the lesson's objective
   B. provide measurable objectives
   C. are usually necessary parts of the total objective
   D. detract from the completion of the final objective

10. In planning instructional activity, the SECOND step is to

    A. establish the overall objectives and standards
    B. identify the blocks of learning which constitute the necessary parts of the total objective
    C. develop lesson plans for each period or unit of instruction
    D. determine the personality and intelligence level of assigned students

11. In planning any instructional activity, the FIRST consideration should be to

    A. identify the blocks of learning which make up the overall objective
    B. determine the overall objectives and standards
    C. develop a sequence of training periods
    D. determine aptitudes of the students

12. In developing a lesson plan, which of these would CORRECTLY state the true objective of the lesson?

    A. To develop the student's skill in planning and following a pattern
    B. To explain and demonstrate the principles of planning and following a pattern
    C. To cover the principles of planning and following a pattern
    D. To learn the principles of planning and following a pattern

13. Which statement is TRUE regarding lesson plans?

    A. The use of standard prepared lesson plans for all students is most effective.
    B. Lesson plans should not contain elements of knowledge or skill previously learned.
    C. Lesson plans should clearly state the desired student learning outcomes.
    D. To be effective, lesson plans need not be in written form.

14. Which statement is TRUE about lesson plans?   14._____

    A. A good lesson plan will eliminate the need for a review of earlier lessons.
    B. The lesson should contain new facts, principles, procedures, or skills related to a previous lesson.
    C. The use of a rigidly prepared lesson plan should be used for an instruction.
    D. An effective lesson plan may be only a mental outline.

15. With regard to the characteristics of a well-planned lesson, each lesson should contain   15._____

    A. all the information needed to reach the objective of the training syllabus
    B. only one element of a simple principle, procedure, or skill
    C. new material that is related to the lesson previously presented
    D. information that is independent of earlier lessons

16. Which statement is TRUE regarding lesson plans?   16._____

    A. Rigidly followed lesson plans for all students is most effective for instruction.
    B. Lesson plans should not be directed toward the course objective, only to the lesson objective.
    C. Lesson plans should not contain material or skills previously learned.
    D. To be effective, lesson plans must be in written form.

17. If lesson plans are constructed in a proper manner, they will provide an outline for   17._____

    A. each lesson of the course without regard to the student/instructor relationship
    B. blocks of learning that become progressively larger, in scope
    C. the teaching procedure to be used in a single instructional period
    D. proceeding from the unknown to the known

18. With regard to the use of a lesson plan, which statement is TRUE?   18._____

    A. If the lesson plan is not leading to the desired results, the instructor should change the approach.
    B. A carefully thought-out lesson plan has little or no bearing on achieving teaching success.
    C. A lesson should provide as much information related to the subject as possible.
    D. An approach which has been successful with one group is always successful with another.

19. Which statement is TRUE regarding lesson plans?   19._____

    A. The rigid use of prepared lesson plans for all students is most effective.
    B. Lesson plans should not include review of earlier lessons.
    C. Lesson plans help instructors to keep a constant check on their own activity as well as that of their students.
    D. Lesson plans may be either *mental outlines* or in written form.

20. Which of these should be the FIRST step in preparing a lecture?   20._____

    A. Planning productive classroom activities
    B. Organizing the material
    C. Establishing the objective and desired outcomes
    D. Researching the subject

21. The preferred method for conducting a teaching lecture is to  21.___

    A. memorize the material to be presented
    B. speak extemporaneously from an outline
    C. speak impromptu with a minimum of specifics
    D. read from prepared material

22. Which teaching method provides no accurate means of checking student learning?  22.___
    _____ method.

    A. Lecture                     B. Programmed instruction
    C. Guided discussion           D. Demonstration-performance

23. Which teaching method is particularly suitable for introducing a subject and is the most  23.___
    economical in terms of the time required to present a given amount of material? _____
    method.

    A. Programmed instruction      B. Demonstration-performance
    C. Guided discussion           D. Lecture

24. The teaching lecture is probably BEST delivered by  24.___

    A. reciting memorized material without the aid of a manuscript
    B. speaking extemporaneously from an outline
    C. speaking impromptu without preparation
    D. reading from a typed or written manuscript

25. In the teaching lecture, the use of which of these would detract from the instructor's dig-  25.___
    nity and reflect upon the student's intelligence?

    A. Simple words
    B. Free-and-easy colloquialisms
    C. Picturesque slang
    D. Errors in grammar and vulgarisms

## KEY (CORRECT ANSWERS)

1. C
2. A
3. C
4. D
5. A

6. D
7. B
8. B
9. A
10. B

11. B
12. D
13. C
14. B
15. C

16. D
17. C
18. A
19. C
20. D

21. B
22. A
23. D
24. B
25. D

# TEST 4

DIRECTIONS: Each question or incomplete statement is followed by several suggested answers or completions. Select the one that BEST answers the question or completes the statement. *PRINT THE LETTER OF THE CORRECT ANSWER IN THE SPACE AT THE RIGHT.*

1. The instructor can BEST inspire active student participation in informal lectures through the use of

    A. negative motivations  B. humor
    C. questions  D. visual aids

2. In regard to the teaching lecture, which of these statements is TRUE?

    A. The instructor must develop a keen perception for subtle responses and must be able to interpret the meaning of these reactions.
    B. Delivering the lecture in an extemporaneous or off-hand manner is not recommended.
    C. The teacher receives direct reaction from the student in the form of verbal or motor activity.
    D. New ideas should be introduced in the conclusion of the lesson.

3. The distinguishing characteristic of an informal lecture is the

    A. relative importance of the subject  B. use of visual aids
    C. student's participation  D. lack of a central idea

4. When a guided discussion is being conducted, the instructor should

    A. never use a reverse question in response to a student's question
    B. discourage students from asking questions
    C. make no comments during the discussion
    D. remember that the more intense the discussion and the greater the participation, the more effective the learning will be

5. When it appears students have adequately discussed the ideas presented during a guided discussion, one of the MOST valuable tools an instructor can use is

    A. a written test on the subject discussed
    B. an immediate recess or dismissal of the class
    C. a taped recording of the discussion
    D. an interim summary of what the students accomplished

6. Learning is produced in a guided discussion through the skillful use of

    A. demonstrations  B. lectures  C. negativism  D. questions

7. In preparing questions for a guided discussion, the instructor should remember that the purpose is to

    A. require that students research the topic
    B. evaluate and grade the student's knowledge
    C. bring about discussion to develop an understanding of the subject
    D. get answers to student questions

8. Which statement about the guided discussion method of teaching is TRUE?

    A. The instructor should answer all student questions never reverse or relay the questions to the class.
    B. The more intense the discussion and the greater the participation, the less effective the learning will be.
    C. Students without a background in the subject should be included in the discussion.
    D. Unless the students have some knowledge to exchange with each other, they cannot reach the desired learning outcomes.

9. In a guided discussion, learning is produced through

    A. explanations and demonstrations
    B. discussion of a topic in which students have little or no background
    C. the skillful use of questions
    D. tutorial instruction

10. During an introduction to a new subject, the instructor can more effectively stimulate group discussion by

    A. selecting a subject in which students lack knowledge
    B. creating a generally relaxed, informal atmosphere
    C. delivering a comprehensive lecture
    D. creating an atmosphere of sternness

11. The basic demonstration-performance method of instruction consists of several steps. In proper order, they are

    A. instructor tells -- student does; student tells -- student does; student does -- instructor evaluates
    B. instructor tells -- instructor does; student tells -- instructor does; student tells -- student does; student does -- instructor evaluates
    C. instructor does -- instructor tells; student does -- instructor tells; student does -- student tells; student does -- instructor evaluates
    D. instructor tells -- instructor does; student tells -- instructor does; student does -- instructor evaluates

12. What are the essential steps in the demonstration-performance method of teaching?

    A. Demonstration, practice, and evaluation
    B. Motivation, presentation, summary, and closure
    C. Explanation, demonstration, student performance, instructor supervision, and evaluation
    D. Demonstration, student performance, and evaluation

13. In the demonstration-performance method of instruction, which two separate actions are performed concurrently?

    A. Instructor demonstration and evaluation
    B. Student performance and instructor evaluation
    C. Instructor explanation and evaluation
    D. Instructor explanation and student demonstration

14. If, due to some unanticipated circumstances, the instructor's demonstration does not conform to the explanation, the instructor should

    A. lower the standards when the student performs the task
    B. *downplay* or ignore the discrepancy as being unimportant to the demonstration
    C. disguise the discrepancy with unrelated instruction
    D. immediately acknowledge and explain the discrepancy

15. Instructional aids used in the teaching-learning process should be

    A. self-supporting and should require no explanation
    B. selected prior to developing and organizing the lesson plan
    C. used to supplant the instructor's oral presentation of a lesson
    D. concentrated on the key points of the lesson

16. The use of instructional aids should be based on their ability to support a specific point in the lesson.
    What is the FIRST step to determine if and where instructional aids are necessary?

    A. Decide at what point in the lesson the student's interest must be rekindled.
    B. Clearly establish the lesson objective, being certain what must be communicated.
    C. Gather necessary data by researching for support material.
    D. Organize subject material into an outline or a lesson plan.

17. Instructional aids used in the teaching-learning process should NOT be used

    A. if detailed schematics are necessary to explain elaborate equipment
    B. as a crutch by the instructor
    C. for teaching more in less time
    D. in conjunction with verbal presentations

18. An instructor cannot retain the reputation of a professional if that person

    A. accepts students as they are with all their faults and problems
    B. does not demand higher pay
    C. instructs on a part-time basis
    D. gives the impression that interest in instruction is secondary to other activities

19. Which personal habit of an instructor is perhaps the MOST important one that affects the professional image?

    A. Common courtesy
    B. Manner of speech
    C. Attire
    D. Personal cleanliness

20. Which of these will make it impossible for the instructor to command the interested attention of the student?

    A. Limiting actions and decisions to standard patterns and practices
    B. Hiding some inadequacy behind a smokescreen of unrelated instruction
    C. Creating a relaxed, informal atmosphere in the classroom
    D. Insisting on correct techniques and procedures from the outset of training

## KEY (CORRECT ANSWERS)

1. C
2. D
3. C
4. D
5. D
6. D
7. C
8. D
9. C
10. B
11. B
12. C
13. B
14. D
15. B
16. B
17. B
18. D
19. D
20. B

# EXAMINATION SECTION
## TEST 1

DIRECTIONS: Each question or incomplete statement is followed by several suggested answers or completions. Select the one that BEST answers the question or completes the statement. *PRINT THE LETTER OF THE CORRECT ANSWER IN THE SPACE AT THE RIGHT.*

1. The LARGEST percentage of a normal person's knowledge is acquired through which of these senses?

    A. Sight
    B. Smell and taste
    C. Touch
    D. Hearing

2. Which of these learning experiences would be the MOST effective in the learning process?

    A. Those which present a minimum challenge to the student
    B. Experiences which involve the student's feelings, thoughts, and memories of past experiences
    C. Experiences which are totally new and unrelated to the learner's previous experiences
    D. Those in which the student need only commit something to memory

3. A student's readiness to learn and understanding of the requirements involved in the learning situation are affected MOST by the

    A. student's intellectual level
    B. student's past experiences
    C. degree of difficulty involved in learning
    D. goals and incentives of other students in the class

4. Learning is strengthened when accompanied by a pleasant or satisfying feeling. This principle is the law of

    A. intensity    B. recency    C. effect    D. primacy

5. Which law of learning implies that a student will learn more from the real thing than from a substitute?
The law of

    A. effect    B. recency    C. intensity    D. primacy

6. Things most often repeated are BEST remembered because of which law of learning? Law of

    A. exercise    B. intensity    C. primacy    D. recency

7. Which law of learning is recognized when an instructor carefully plans a summary school lesson or a critique? Law of

    A. intensity    B. recency    C. effect    D. exercise

8. If a student has a strong purpose, a clear objective, and a well-fixed reason for learning something, it is the result of the law of

    A. readiness    B. effect    C. intensity    D. primacy

9. The law of _____ learning states that learning is weakened when associated with an unpleasant feeling.

   A. readiness   B. primacy   C. intensity   D. effect

10. If students lack-motivation, their-progress will be LESS than if the law of _____ learning prevails.

    A. primacy   B. exercise   C. effect   D. readiness

11. Teaching the student to perform a task right the first time is an example of the law of

    A. readiness   B. recency   C. effect   D. primacy

12. The law of exercise is the basis of

    A. learning by rote
    B. the emotional reaction of the learner
    C. learning to do things right the first time
    D. practice and drill

13. A basic need that affects all of a person's perceptions is the need to

    A. avoid areas of any threat to success
    B. accomplish a higher level of learning
    C. maintain and enhance the person's own organized self
    D. acquire a formal education

14. What is the basis of all learning?

    A. Motivation                B. Perception
    C. Positive self-concept     D. Insight

15. Instruction, as opposed to the *trial and error* method of learning, is desirable because competent instruction speeds the learning process by

    A. teaching the relationship of perceptions as they occur
    B. relieving the student of the task of self-evaluation
    C. eliminating the practice of exploring and experimenting
    D. emphasizing only the important points of training

16. Which statement is TRUE about the perceptual process?

    A. Negative self-concepts have little or no effect on the perceptual process.
    B. An individual's beliefs and value structures have no effect on perceptions.
    C. All perceptions are affected by the need to preserve and perpetuate one's self.
    D. Fear favorably affects perceptions by widening a person's perceptual field.

17. *Insights,* as applied to learning, involve a person's

    A. awareness of those processes which are not immediately apparent
    B. grouping of associated perceptions into meaningful wholes
    C. ability to recognize the reason for learning a procedure
    D. self-concept or self-image

18. Perceptions result when a person 18._____

    A. responds to visual cues first, then aural cues, and relates these cues to ones previously learned
    B. groups together bits of information
    C. gives meaning to sensations being experienced
    D. responds correctly to self-evaluation

19. In the learning process, fear or the element of threat will 19._____

    A. accelerate the attainment of perceptions
    B. improve the student's ability to cope with the learning situation
    C. narrow the student's perceptual field
    D. intensify the student's desire to improve performance

20. Evoking student insights is one of the instructor's major responsibilities. 20._____
    This involves

    A. the grouping of perceptions into meaningful wholes
    B. a student's immediate grasp of theoretical principles as they are taught in school
    C. the analysis of a student by the instructor
    D. the ability of a student to master the rote performance of a task that has been learned

21. To predict how the student will interpret training experiences and instructions, the instructor must have knowledge of the student's 21._____

    A. intelligence and previous educational accomplishments
    B. readiness to learn
    C. basic need to maintain and enhance one's organized self
    D. precise kinds of commitments and philosophical outlooks

22. To enhance the instructor's relationship with students, an instructor should be aware that students have 22._____

    A. a tendency to shirk responsibility, because people are inherently lazy
    B. relinquished their role as individuals while enrolled in training programs
    C. drives and desires that they continually try to satisfy in one way or the other
    D. feelings of insecurity when receiving criticism, whether constructive or not

23. Select the TRUE statement concerning negative self-concepts. 23._____
    Negative self-concepts

    A. should be considered an asset to learning because they favorably affect the *ability to do*
    B. may be used to the advantage of an instructor who has a good understanding of psychology
    C. may inhibit the ability of the student to properly implement that which is perceived
    D. may be helpful because positive experiences often tend to contradict or destroy the self-concept

24. The student who has negative experiences which tend to contradict self-concepts is PROBABLY one who  24.____

   A. compensates for a personality conflict with the instructor
   B. attempts to suppress aggressive reactions
   C. will tend to reject instruction
   D. is psychologically motivated for further training

25. An instructor may foster the development of insights by  25.____

   A. introducing the student to at least two new tasks during each lesson
   B. always keeping the rate of learning consistent so that it is predictable
   C. pointing out the attractive features of the activity to be learned
   D. helping the student acquire and maintain a favorable self-concept

## KEY (CORRECT ANSWERS)

| | | | |
|---|---|---|---|
| 1. | A | 11. | B |
| 2. | B | 12. | A |
| 3. | B | 13. | C |
| 4. | C | 14. | B |
| 5. | C | 15. | D |
| 6. | A | 16. | C |
| 7. | A | 17. | B |
| 8. | D | 18. | C |
| 9. | D | 19. | D |
| 10. | D | 20. | A |

21. C
22. C
23. B
24. C
25. D

# TEST 2

DIRECTIONS: Each question or incomplete statement is followed by several suggested answers or completions. Select the one that BEST answers the question or completes the statement. *PRINT THE LETTER OF THE CORRECT ANSWER IN THE SPACE AT THE RIGHT.*

1. The factor which contributes MOST to a student's failure to remain receptive to new experiences or which creates a tendency to reject additional training is the student's 1.____

   A. physical organism  B. goals and values
   C. basic needs  D. negative self-concept

2. Select the CORRECT statement pertaining to motivation. 2.____

   A. The desire for personal gain is a form of negative motivation.
   B. Slumps in learning are often due to slumps in motivation.
   C. Motivation has little to do with learning.
   D. Negative motivations are as effective in promoting efficient learning as are positive motivations.

3. Which of these is a form of negative motivation? 3.____

   A. Reproof and threats
   B. The promise of achievement of rewards
   C. The belief that success is possible under certain circumstances
   D. Realizing that certain actions and operations may prevent injury or loss of life

4. Which of the following is *generally* the MORE effective way for the instructor to properly motivate students? 4.____

   A. Reinforce their self-confidence by requiring no tasks beyond their ability to perform
   B. Appeal to their pride and self-esteem
   C. Provide positive motivations by the promise or achievement of rewards
   D. Maintain pleasant personal relationships with students, even though it may be necessary to lower standards at times

5. Which of these may produce fears and be accepted by the student as threats? _____ motivations. 5.____

   A. Negative  B. Positive
   C. Intangible  D. Tangible

6. Motivations in the form of reproof and threats should be avoided with all but the student who is 6.____

   A. slow or discouraged
   B. bored or disinterested
   C. overconfident and impulsive
   D. timid and shy

7. Which statement is TRUE concerning motivations? 7.____

   A. Negative motivations characteristically are as effective as positive motivations.
   B. Motivations may be very subtle and difficult to identify.

C. There is little or no motivation in menial tasks such as digging a ditch.
D. Motivations must be tangible to be effective.

8. What effect does making each lesson a pleasurable experience have on the student?  8.___

   A. Fosters complacency
   B. Maintains a high level of motivation
   C. Tends to lower standards of performance
   D. Develops undesirable habit patterns

9. To promote efficient learning, the instructor should use  9.___

   A. positive and negative motivators as equally as possible
   B. positive motivators rather than negative motivators
   C. negative motivators more often than positive motivators
   D. only negative motivators

10. The dominant force which governs the student's progress and ability to learn is  10.___

    A. physical organism         B. insight
    C. perception                D. motivation

11. An instructor can MOST effectively maintain a high level of student motivation by  11.___

    A. setting performance standards to match the student's ability
    B. making things easy for the student
    C. making each lesson a pleasant experience for the student
    D. conducting lessons which offer no rewards

12. The HIGHEST level of learning has been achieved when a person is able to  12.___

    A. accomplish or perform each element of a procedure precisely
    B. accurately repeat verbally what has been learned
    C. understand each segment of a particular subject, procedure, or technique
    D. correlate an element which has been learned with other segments or blocks of learning or accomplishments

13. A person who has learned by rote is one who  13.___

    A. can repeat back something which has been taught, without being able to understand what has been learned
    B. understands what has been taught
    C. has achieved the skill to apply what has been taught
    D. is able to associate an element which has been learned with other segments of learning

14. The LOWEST level of learning has been attained when the student  14.___

    A. can repeat back something without understanding what has been learned
    B. understands what has been taught
    C. can apply what has been taught
    D. can associate an element which has been learned with other segments of learning

15. A leveling-off process or *learning plateau* in a student's progress is considered      15.____

    A. normal and should be expected after an initial period of rapid improvement
    B. abnormal since it means that learning has ceased
    C. abnormal and should not be brought to the student's attention
    D. normal if it does not stay level for significant periods of effort

16. On a graph showing the typical progress in learning, the initial leveling off of the learning      16.____
    curve is called a

    A. learning plateau           B. progress reversal
    C. learning gradient          D. progress advance

17. Which of these would be MOST profitable to a beginning student?      17.____

    A. Assignment of a grade on performance
    B. Evaluation of performance against a set standard
    C. Early evaluation to predict eventual proficiency
    D. Constructive critique to help eliminate errors

18. Which of the following would MOST likely be an indication that a student is reacting      18.____
    abnormally to stress?

    A. Automatic response to a given situation
    B. Extreme overcooperation
    C. Slow progress
    D. Hesitancy to act

19. The instructor can counteract anxiety in a student by      19.____

    A. ignoring the student's fears
    B. treating the student's fears as a normal reaction
    C. continuously citing the unhappy consequences of faulty performance
    D. discontinuing instruction in the tasks that cause anxiety

20. One of the SUREST ways to lose the student's confidence and attention is for the      20.____
    instructor to

    A. admit not knowing the answer to the student's question
    B. create the impression of *talking down* to the student
    C. acknowledge that both the student and instructor are important to each other
    D. refer to a checklist

21. Which of the following would MOST likely be an indication that a student is reacting      21.____
    abnormally to stress?

    A. Inappropriate laughter or singing
    B. Rapid thinking and reaction
    C. Automatic response to a given situation
    D. Slow changes in emotions

22. What technique can the instructor use to delay the onset of fatigue during class instruction?  22.____

    A. Introducing a number of different thoughts involving different theories and objectives
    B. Increasing the complexity of problems
    C. Lengthening the instruction periods
    D. Increasing the frequency of instruction periods

23. Which of the following is the MOST accurate statement concerning student concentration during classroom instruction?  23.____
    Concentration

    A. will be more pronounced when a number of tasks involving different elements and objectives are introduced
    B. is the primary consideration in determining the length and frequency of instruction periods
    C. is induced solely because of tenseness and can be minimized by a review of tasks already learned
    D. is a factor which depends more on mental alertness than on physical condition

24. When under stress, normal individuals USUALLY react  24.____

    A. by responding rapidly and exactly, often automatically, within the limits of their experience and training
    B. inappropriately such as extreme overcooperation, painstaking self-control, and inappropriate laughing or singing
    C. with very rapid changes in emotions, severe anger at the instructor, or others
    D. with marked changes in mood on different lessons such as excellent morale followed by deep depression

25. Which of the following would lead to lack of student confidence in the instructor?  25.____

    A. Too much help and encouragement given by the instructor to the slow student
    B. Unplanned periods of instruction or poor preparation
    C. A situation in which quick or brisk instruction is given
    D. An examination given on the first day of class

## KEY (CORRECT ANSWERS)

| | | | |
|---|---|---|---|
| 1. | D | 11. | C |
| 2. | B | 12. | D |
| 3. | A | 13. | A |
| 4. | D | 14. | A |
| 5. | A | 15. | A |
| 6. | C | 16. | A |
| 7. | B | 17. | D |
| 8. | B | 18. | D |
| 9. | B | 19. | B |
| 10. | D | 20. | B |

21. A
22. A
23. B
24. A
25. B

# TEST 3

DIRECTIONS: Each question or incomplete statement is followed by several suggested answers or completions. Select the one that BEST answers the question or completes the statement. *PRINT THE LETTER OF THE CORRECT ANSWER IN THE SPACE AT THE RIGHT.*

1. To deal with the problem of a sick student, the instructor should be aware that it is      1.____

    A. confined to the emotionally unstable student
    B. a temporary illness
    C. a reaction to apprehension that is only exhibited by the failing student
    D. due to a lack of confidence on the student's part

2. Students who grow impatient when learning the basic elements of a task are those who      2.____

    A. should have the preliminary training presented one step at a time with clearly stated goals for each step
    B. are less easily discouraged than the unaggressive students
    C. possess superior motivation
    D. should not be held back by insisting that the immediate goal be reached before they progress to the next step

3. Instruction that is keyed to the pace of a slow learner, but is applied to an apt student, will MOST likely result in      3.____

    A. anxiety
    B. confusion
    C. impatience
    D. a feeling of unfair evaluations

4. According to one theory, some forgetting is due to the practice of submerging an unpleasant experience into the subconscious.
   This is called      4.____

    A. repression                B. disuse
    C. interference              D. blanking

5. Concerning the factors involved in remembering, which statement is TRUE?      5.____

    A. Negativism promotes remembering.
    B. Repetition guarantees remembering.
    C. Practice guarantees remembering.
    D. Praise stimulates remembering.

6. One theory about forgetting is that an item is forgotten because a later experience has overshadowed it.
   This process is called      6.____

    A. repression                B. disuse
    C. interference              D. blanking

7. Which of these BEST ensures recall of material on tasks that have been taught?    7.____

   A. Practice of mere repetition
   B. Rote learning
   C. Meaningful teaching
   D. Negative motivations

8. Things learned previously by the student may either help or hinder the current learning task.    8.____
   This process GENERALLY is called

   A. insight            B. interference
   C. transfer of learning    D. correlation

9. Which statement is TRUE about transfer of learning?    9.____

   A. Positive transfer occurs if the learning of one skill interferes with retention or proficiency of another skill.
   B. Negative transfer occurs when students interpret new things in terms of what they already know.
   C. Positive transfer occurs when the learning of one skill helps the student learn another skill.
   D. Negative transfer occurs when the process refutes the interference theory of forgetting.

10. To ensure further learning and correct student performance after the completion of a course, it is the instructor's responsibility to    10.____

    A. allow incorrect performance at the beginning of the course to *get those errors out of the student's system*
    B. proceed to the next learning task even though the more simple tasks are performed incorrectly
    C. accept improper habits during the early phase of the course and correct these faults later
    D. insist on correct techniques and procedures from the outset of the course

11. To help the student achieve transfer of learning, the instructor should    11.____

    A. make certain the student understands that what is learned can be applied to other situations
    B. encourage rote learning
    C. discourage the use of imagination and ingenuity in applying knowledge and skills
    D. use instructional materials that precludes the formation of well-founded concepts and generalizations

12. Which generalization about motivated human nature has been made by noted psychologists?    12.____

    A. A human being will not exercise self-direction and self-control in the pursuit of committed goals.
    B. The average human being does not inherently dislike work.
    C. It is human nature to shirk responsibility.
    D. The capacity to exercise a relatively high degree of imagination, ingenuity, and creativity in solving common problems is rare in the human race.

13. Before a student can concentrate on learning, which of the human needs must be satisfied?  13.____

    A. Self-fulfillment    B. Safety
    C. Social              D. Physical

14. Which of the student's human needs offers the GREATEST challenge to the instructor?  14.____

    A. Self-fulfillment    B. Physical
    C. Safety              D. Social

15. Among the various human needs, the individual is FIRST concerned with  15.____

    A. personal safety     B. social needs
    C. self-fulfillment    D. physical needs

16. After individuals are physically comfortable and have no fear for their safety, _____ needs become the PRIME influence on their behavior.  16.____

    A. social              B. egoistic
    C. materialistic       D. physical

17. When a student becomes bewildered and lost in the advanced phase of learning after completing the early phase without grasping the fundamentals, the defense mechanism is USUALLY in the form of  17.____

    A. rationalization     B. aggression
    C. flight              D. resignation

18. When students display the defense mechanism called aggression, they  18.____

    A. attempt to justify actions that otherwise would be unacceptable
    B. may refuse to participate in the activities of the class
    C. develop symptoms or ailments that give them satisfactory excuses for removing themselves from frustration
    D. become so frustrated they lose interest and give up

19. When students subconsciously use the defense mechanism called rationalization, they  19.____

    A. develop symptoms that give them excuses for removing themselves from frustration
    B. cannot accept the real reasons for their behavior
    C. become aggressive against something or somebody
    D. no longer believe it profitable or even possible to work further

20. When students become so frustrated they no longer believe it profitable or even possible to work further, they USUALLY display which defense mechanism?  20.____

    A. Resignation         B. Aggression
    C. Escape              D. Rationalization

21. Taking physical or mental flight is a defense mechanism that students use when they  21.____

    A. want to escape from frustrating situations
    B. cannot accept the real reasons for their behavior

C. become bewildered and lost in the advanced phase of training
D. attempt to justify actions that otherwise would be unacceptable

22. Although defense mechanisms can serve a useful purpose, they also can be hindrances because they  22.____

    A. destroy feelings of failure
    B. alleviate the causes of problems
    C. provide feelings of adequacy
    D. involve self-deception and distortion of reality

23. When a student uses excuses to justify inadequate performance, it is an indication of the defense mechanism known as  23.____

    A. escape
    B. rationalization
    C. aggression
    D. resignation

24. When a student asks irrelevant questions or refuses to participate in class activities, it USUALLY is an indication of the defense mechanism known as  24.____

    A. escape
    B. rationalization
    C. aggression
    D. resignation

25. When a student engages in daydreaming, it is the defense mechanism of  25.____

    A. escape
    B. rationalization
    C. aggression
    D. resignation

## KEY (CORRECT ANSWERS)

| | | | |
|---|---|---|---|
| 1. | B | 11. | A |
| 2. | A | 12. | B |
| 3. | C | 13. | D |
| 4. | A | 14. | A |
| 5. | C | 15. | A |
| 6. | B | 16. | C |
| 7. | C | 17. | D |
| 8. | C | 18. | A |
| 9. | C | 19. | B |
| 10. | D | 20. | C |

21. C
22. D
23. B
24. C
25. A

# TEST 4

DIRECTIONS: Each question or incomplete statement is followed by several suggested answers or completions. Select the one that BEST answers the question or completes the statement. *PRINT THE LETTER OF THE CORRECT ANSWER IN THE SPACE AT THE RIGHT.*

1. Which statement is TRUE regarding true professionalism as an instructor?  1.___

    A. To achieve professionalism, actions and decisions must be limited to standard patterns and practices.
    B. Anything less than sincere performance destroys the effectiveness of the professional instructor.
    C. Professionalism is not necessarily based on intelligence or the ability to reason logically and accurately.
    D. A single definition of professionalism would encompass all of the qualifications and considerations which must be present.

2. Student confidence tends to be destroyed if instructors  2.___

    A. identify the student's errors and failures
    B. bluff whenever in doubt about some point
    C. acknowledge their own mistakes
    D. direct and control the student's actions and behavior

3. The professional relationship between the instructor and the student should be based upon the  3.___

    A. mutual acknowledgement that they are important to each other and both are working toward the same objective
    B. concept that making things easy for the student and accepting lower standards will improve the relationship
    C. need to disregard the student's personal faults, interests, or problems
    D. understanding that during the training course, the instructor's objectives are different from the student's

4. Which of these would MORE likely result in students becoming frustrated?  4.___

    A. Telling the students that their work is unsatisfactory with no explanation
    B. Neglecting to tell students what is expected of them and what they can expect
    C. Failing to point out to students how a particular lesson or course can help them reach an important goal
    D. Covering up instructor mistakes or bluffing when the instructor is in doubt

5. In the communication process, the communicator will be more successful in gaining and retaining the receiver's attention by  5.___

    A. varying the communicative approach
    B. providing an atmosphere which discourages questioning
    C. presenting the message in a manner that is totally foreign to the receiver's experiences
    D. relying on technical language to express ideas to the receiver

6. Which statement is TRUE regarding effective communication during student instruction? Effective communication

    A. has taken place when information is provided in such a way that it changes the behavior of the student
    B. has taken place when the student is able to repeat the information that has been received
    C. is when the student has accurately received the information even though the factors and principles are not yet understood
    D. at its best is when information is accurately transmitted and received

7. To communicate *effectively,* instructors must

    A. depend on a highly technical or professional background to ensure acceptance of the message
    B. reveal a positive and confident attitude while delivering their message
    C. rely on technical language to express ideas clearly to students
    D. limit the method of communication to one channel (hearing, seeing, or feeling) to avoid confusion

8. In the communication process, if a listener has difficulty in understanding the symbols the speaker is using, and indicates confusion, the speaker

    A. is encouraged and force is added to communication
    B. should avoid the use of concrete words
    C. should resort to the use of abstract words
    D. may become puzzled and uncertain

9. In the communication process, a speaker is encouraged and force is added to communication when the listener

    A. has difficulty in understanding and indicates confusion
    B. reacts favorably
    C. shows an attitude of passive neutrality
    D. has no experiences in common with the speaker

10. Effective communication has taken place when, and only when, the

    A. sender uses a vocabulary (written or oral) that is meaningful to the reader or listener
    B. communicator has convinced the listener there is a need to know the ideas presented
    C. receiver has the ability to question and comprehend the ideas that have been transmitted
    D. receivers react with understanding and change their behavior accordingly

11. The effectiveness of communication between the instructor and the student is measured by the

    A. facial expressions of the student during a lesson
    B. similarity between the idea transmitted and the idea received
    C. degree of attention the student gives to the instructor during a lesson
    D. level of motivation displayed by the student

12. Probably the GREATEST single barrier to effective communication in the teaching process is a lack of

    A. personality harmony between instructor and student
    B. quiet environment
    C. time available for communication
    D. a common experience level between the instructor and student

13. By the use of abstractions in the communication process, the communicator will

    A. narrow and gain better control of the image produced in the minds of listeners and readers
    B. not evoke in the listener's or reader's mind the specific items of experience the communicator intends
    C. be using words which refer to objects or ideas that human beings can experience directly
    D. bring forth specific items of experience in the minds of the receivers

14. Probably the GREATEST single barrier to effective communication is the

    A. confusion between the symbol and the thing symbolized
    B. making of statements which contain inaccuracies
    C. use of abstractions by the communicator
    D. lack of a common core of experience between communicator and receiver

15. A communicator's words cannot communicate the desired meaning to another person unless the

    A. listener or reader has had some experience with the objects or concepts to which these words refer
    B. words give the meaning that is in the mind of the receiver
    C. communicator makes extensive use of abstractions
    D. communicator avoids the use of words which relate to the receiver's past experience

16. The danger in using abstract words is that they

    A. will not evoke the specific items of experience in the listener's mind that the communicator intends
    B. control the image produced in the listener's mind
    C. refer only to things that people are familiar with or can relate to
    D. are overly concise in their meanings

17. Instructors who limit their thinking to the whole group without considering the individuals within that group are

    A. using a good lecture technique
    B. assuming all students have an average personality which really fits no one
    C. presenting information efficiently for maximum retention
    D. using an excellent time-saving measure

18. Which of the following is one of the ways in which anxiety or apprehension will affect a student? Anxiety

    A. tends to increase mental acuity and perceptiveness, but interferes with muscular coordination
    B. causes dispersal of the student's attention over such a wide range of matters as to interfere with normal reactions
    C. will speed up the learning process for the student if properly controlled and directed by the instructor
    D. may limit the student's ability to learn from perceptions

19. Faulty performance due to student overconfidence should be corrected by

    A. requiring the student to perform unpleasant tasks
    B. raising the standard of performance for each lesson
    C. withholding the evaluation of the student's progress
    D. praising the student only when it is deserved

20. Ridicule and reproof of a slow and apprehensive student is

    A. effective if the student understands the reason for being criticized in this manner
    B. ineffective in encouraging learning
    C. generally an effective psychological tool because students will work to avoid unpleasant experiences
    D. effective because students learn best when mistakes are pointed out in a forceful manner

21. When a student correctly understands the situation and knows the correct procedure for the task, but fails to act at the proper time, the student MOST probably

    A. will be unable to cope with the demands of the task
    B. is handicapped by indifference or lack of interest
    C. feels that the instructor is making unreasonable demands for performance and progress
    D. lacks self-confidence

22. What should an instructor do if a student's slow progress is due to discouragement and a lack of confidence?

    A. Assign subgoals which can be attained more easily than the normal learning goals
    B. Provide unlimited help and encouragement
    C. Raise the performance standards so that the student will gain satisfaction in meeting higher standards
    D. Emphasize the negative aspects of poor performance by pointing out the serious consequences

23. If a student's progress is slow due to discouragement and a lack of confidence, the instructor should

    A. provide unlimited help and encouragement
    B. accept the slow rate of progress and accept a substandard performance
    C. have the student practice elements of the task involved until confidence and ability are gained
    D. discontinue directing the student's attention to the unacceptable performance

24. The *usual* result when a student has made an earnest effort but is told that the work is not satisfactory, with no other explanation, is   24.___

    A. increased effort
    B. frustration
    C. regression
    D. increased motivation

25. When the instructor keeps the student informed of lesson objectives and completion standards, it minimizes the student's   25.___

    A. individuality
    B. insecurity
    C. motivation
    D. aggressiveness

## KEY (CORRECT ANSWERS)

| | | | |
|---|---|---|---|
| 1. B | | 11. D | |
| 2. B | | 12. D | |
| 3. A | | 13. C | |
| 4. B | | 14. D | |
| 5. A | | 15. A | |
| 6. D | | 16. A | |
| 7. B | | 17. B | |
| 8. D | | 18. D | |
| 9. B | | 19. D | |
| 10. B | | 20. B | |
| | 21. D | | |
| | 22. A | | |
| | 23. C | | |
| | 24. B | | |
| | 25. B | | |

# EXAMINATION SECTION
# TEST 1

DIRECTIONS: Each question or incomplete statement is followed by several suggested answers or completions. Select the one that BEST answers the question or completes the statement. *PRINT THE LETTER OF THE CORRECT ANSWER IN THE SPACE AT THE RIGHT.*

1. The MOST desirable type of classroom discipline is BEST attained through which one of the following practices?  1.____

    A. Encouraging traits of self-discipline
    B. Including class behavior in the final rating
    C. Establishing the idea that rules and regulations will be strictly enforced
    D. Anticipating difficulty and sending the first few minor cases of breach of discipline to the chairman or dean
    E. Maintaining a permissive or a restrictive atmosphere in the classroom but never a mixture of both

2. If you find a student in one of your classes doing very poorly despite an obviously high potential, the MOST desirable procedure among the following to take is to  2.____

    A. refer the student to the guidance counselor
    B. ask the student to bring his parents to school to see you
    C. write a letter to his parents asking them to come to school to see you
    D. interview the student yourself before making any referrals or calling his parents
    E. fail him

3. The procedure of requiring students to stand and face the class when responding is  3.____

    A. *advisable* because it discourages calling out of answers
    B. *inadvisable* because it creates an ordeal for the shy student
    C. *advisable* because it increases audibility of answers
    D. *inadvisable* because a recalcitrant student would dispute the rule
    E. *advisable* because it trains the class in the American way of standing up and facing an adversary eye to eye

4. Of the following, the BEST procedure for obtaining the aim of a specific lesson is  4.____

    A. for the teacher to state the aim of the lesson and write it on the blackboard so that all will be sure to have it
    B. to elicit the aim from the class and have it written on the board
    C. for the teacher to dictate the aim of the lesson so that all students can get it in their notebooks
    D. to give the aim the previous day so that the students can prepare for the lesson
    E. to secure a class consensus on the aim by secret vote

5. Of the following, the BEST course of action for a new teacher who is having difficulty in presenting a particular type of lesson to take is to  5.____

    A. make an arrangement with an experienced teacher to observe his classes
    B. consult the chairman and request an opportunity for intervisitation
    C. try to adjust without outside help to avoid demonstrating weakness to colleagues

D. discuss the problem frankly with the class and ask for suggestions from the class
E. take in-service courses

6. Of the following, the BEST situation for using essay questions is where

   A. it is desired to test the ability of a pupil to organize his answers
   B. the class is made up chiefly of slow pupils
   C. *single shot* questions are needed to complete an examination
   D. it is desired to sample a large area of subject matter
   E. it is desired to sample a small area of subject matter

7. In a lesson in which a new topic is to be taught, which one of the following is the MOST desirable principle to follow?

   A. Make certain that all difficulties encountered by pupils in doing the previous homework assignment have been corrected before beginning the new topic.
   B. Allow sufficient time to include a suitable motivation of the new material, a development, and independent pupil practice.
   C. Introduce the new topic, but require pupils to study the textbook for a complete explanation.
   D. Insist that no questions be asked by pupils until the development is completed.
   E. Permit all students who have not completed the previous topic to continue on it and require only those who show the requisite ability and interest to take up the new topic.

8. A test may be said to be reliable when

   A. it consistently measures what it purports to measure
   B. it adequately deals with the types of educational outcomes to be measured at proper levels of difficulty for pupils
   C. there is a high correlation between test scores and criterion measures
   D. it can be obtained on time from publishers
   E. it measures accurately whatever it does measure

9. Of the following, the one which does NOT measure the concentration of scores in any set of scores or group of data is the

   A. mode     B. modulus     C. mean     D. median     E. middle

10. Of the following, the GREATEST advantage of short-answer tests is the

    A. ease with which the test items can be constructed
    B. ease with which such tests can be standardized
    C. wide sampling of the subject matter of the course
    D. ease with which the test results can be interpreted
    E. large number of questions that can be given as contrasted with the essay test

11. The MOST effective use of the talents and abilities of the able pupils in your subject area would be gained by which one of the following procedures?

    A. Give them extra homework assignments in order to earn better marks.
    B. Give them the responsibility of tutoring disadvantaged pupils.
    C. Give them monitorial duties, such as marking test papers.

D. Excuse them from class work which they grasp easily so they do enrichment work in other subject areas.
E. Have them serve as the teacher in as many class situations as possible.

12. The MAIN advantage of standardized tests is    12.____

    A. objectivity
    B. ease of marking for teachers
    C. marks may be compared with other groups
    D. it provides greater motivation for students
    E. they are held *secure*

13. A percentile score of 55 is    13.____

    A. a score equivalent to the arithmetic median of the scores
    B. equaled or exceeded by 45% of the scores in the distribution
    C. equivalent to a score of 55 out of 100
    D. the accepted norm
    E. equivalent to a raw score of 55

14. The process of reviewing homework daily is time-consuming. Of the following suggestions made by a group of teachers, which one is MOST sound pedagogically?    14.____

    A. Do not go over the homework at all.
    B. Go over, in class, only the problems with which pupils had trouble.
    C. Collect the homework of only one row at a time and return it corrected the next day.
    D. Collect the homework of the whole class once a week on a specific day.
    E. Before going on to the new lesson, be sure to go over all the homework.

15. Which one of the following is the BEST statement about a teacher's technique of questioning?    15.____

    A. No question should be so difficult that even the slowest pupil couldn't answer it.
    B. Each lesson should have at least one question which would require the pupils to do critical thinking.
    C. There should be a series of pivotal questions to highlight the chief learnings.
    D. Each question should be simple and short.
    E. At times, use the *whiplash* or *tugging* types with slow learners.

16. Of the following, the BEST statement concerning skill in questioning is that    16.____

    A. to make sure all students hear, the teacher should often repeat her question
    B. answers should be repeated because some children sit far away from the pupil who is answering
    C. each question should be addressed to a particular pupil by giving his name before asking the question
    D. to vary the kinds of questions, include the double question, particularly for bright students
    E. a question should be addressed to the entire class

17. Of the following, the LEAST effective method for obtaining pupil participation is to    17.____

A. give a warm-up drill to the entire class
B. group the class and give different assignments to each group
C. have pupils answer in concert
D. use experiences of pupils in the lesson development
E. ask thought-provoking pivotal questions

18. A test which is TOO difficult will usually yield scores that fall into a _____ distribution.

    A. bell-shaped
    B. negatively skewed
    C. positively skewed
    D. bimodal
    E. variety of patterns of

19. The MOST desirable routine procedure for going over homework is to

    A. compare answers orally with the class
    B. have students put their work on the board and explain it to the rest of the class
    C. have the teacher do each example together with the class
    D. collect it and mark it outside of class, returning it within a week
    E. ask students to raise their hands if they have the correct answer as it is announced by the teacher

20. Of the following characteristics of a good lesson plan, the one which applies LEAST is that it

    A. forms part of a larger unit
    B. helps give direction to the lesson
    C. be adhered to even if vital side issues appear
    D. focuses on a meaningful problem
    E. refers to previous lessons and learnings

21. The degree to which a test measures what it is supposed to measure is called its

    A. validity
    B. coefficient of correlation
    C. objectivity
    D. reliability
    E. consistency

22. Of the following audio-visual aids, the one that represents a MOST recent innovation in science teaching is

    A. single topic films
    B. film strips
    C. 2x2 inch colored slides
    D. 16 mm sound films
    E. 8 mm sound films

23. Of the following reasons for using charts as a teaching device in the classroom, the MOST desirable one is the

    A. ease with which large numbers of charts can be stored
    B. ability to use color for both functional and decorative effect
    C. ability to include many details about a topic on one chart
    D. ability to make comparisons between various things, places, distances, conditions, etc.
    E. ease with which they can be followed in a class discussion

24. Of the following techniques employed in questioning, the one that probably has the LEAST value for conceptual learning would be questions of a type that are  24.____

    A. varied in difficulty and directed to appropriate pupils
    B. rapid-fire and call for monosyllabic responses
    C. pivotal in nature and call for analysis
    D. questions of pupils that are directed back to other pupils by the teacher
    E. based on *why* rather than on *what*

25. Of the following reasons for including essay questions in an examination, the one that is probably MOST important is that this type of question  25.____

    A. provides greater coverage of material than other test items
    B. is easier to formulate than good objective-type questions
    C. provides opportunities for subjective evaluation of answers
    D. provides for pupil expression in an organized manner and in depth
    E. emphasizes thinking through rather than mere recall

26. Of the following practices for helping a beginning teacher in the classroom, the BEST would probably be to  26.____

    A. have informal discussions with colleagues at opportune times
    B. continue taking courses at the local colleges
    C. follow a planned program of intervisitation
    D. attend departmental conferences devoted to pedagogy
    E. ask the principal or chairman to sit in on his first month of teaching

27. Of the following reasons for using, at times, a single loop movie projector rather than a 16 mm movie projector, the one reason that is INCORRECT is that it(s)  27.____

    A. is faster to load and unload film
    B. can be used in a more flexible manner
    C. can be used without darkening the room
    D. sound track can produce sound of functional fidelity
    E. sound track can produce sound of higher fidelity

28. Of the following practices for training students to give reports in class, the one that is LEAST recommended is to  28.____

    A. insist that they read them
    B. limit their reports to a stated time
    C. encourage them to use simple illustrations
    D. permit reference to notes during a presentation
    E. prepare summary questions to test the agreement or understanding of the class

29. Of the following reasons for experimenting with team teaching methods, the one that is probably MOST valid from an educational point of view is that it  29.____

    A. would help meet the problem of teacher shortage
    B. would provide overburdened teachers with more free time
    C. makes provision for flexible scheduling and independent study by pupils
    D. can easily be incorporated into old as well as new school plants
    E. would provide more highly skilled teachers

30. In considering the roles of a homeroom teacher, the one of the following which would probably be considered LEAST important from an educational viewpoint is to

    A. give guidance since the school has licensed guidance counselors
    B. keep accurate and up-to-date records for students
    C. provide a program of tutorial assistance for students that need help
    D. maintain firm discipline while routine school matters are being handled
    E. establish liaison with the parents of the students

31. Of the following practices followed by teachers in doing project work, the one that probably has the LEAST merit is to

    A. require that every student submit an individual project
    B. display class projects in a science fair held in the school
    C. encourage students to work in committees on group projects
    D. provide opportunity for pupils to discuss their work on school time
    E. organize a project center where displays of the best work may be seen

32. If a teacher wanted to prepare seventy copies of a five-page test for two of his classes, he would probably find that the machine which was MOST practical for this purpose is a(n)

    A. polygraph        B. mimeograph        C. kymograph
    D. offset           E. xerox

33. Of the following, the one who was a Harvard psychologist and author of THE PROCESS OF EDUCATION and TOWARD A THEORY OF INSTRUCTION was

    A. James Conant         B. Jerome S. Bruner
    C. John H. Fischer      D. H. Bentley Glass
    E. James M. Hester

34. Of the following types of objective questions, the one that is considered MOST flexible and statistically reliable is the

    A. modified true-false      B. matching
    C. completion               D. multiple choice
    E. true-false

35. Of the following, probably the LEAST valuable way to begin a new topic or lesson is for the teacher to

    A. distribute a step-by-step outline of the topics or lesson
    B. explore some interest already possessed by the student
    C. elicit an explanation of the importance of the subject
    D. develop an overview of the subject
    E. refer to some current event

36. Motivation for a lesson is BEST when it

    A. makes a sharp transition from the previous lesson
    B. is dramatic
    C. raises a question that poses a problem for the class
    D. is succinct
    E. arouses emotions, preferably indignation or dissent .

7 (#1)

37. In administering the Iowa Tests of Educational Development, the one factor among the following that is NOT a primary aim is to

   A. identify the intellectually gifted
   B. show parents the fixed limitations of their children
   C. serve as backgrounds for conferences between parents and counselors
   D. select students for remedial classes
   E. aid in ability grouping

38. The teacher might curtail continued and disturbing conversations during a recitation by doing all of the following EXCEPT

   A. walking around the room, making it a point to stand near potential talkers
   B. separating friends who encourage misbehavior in one another
   C. singling out the talkers and publicly admonishing and embarrassing them
   D. drawing the talkers into the group activity without a special reprimand
   E. motivating interest and participation through thought-provoking questions, cartoons, demonstrations, etc.

39. Of the following, the BEST reason for the assignment of suitable homework is that it provides

   A. each parent with an opportunity to learn what her child is learning
   B. all the necessary follow-up drill for teaching
   C. practice in reading skills
   D. further opportunities for application of skills or concepts taught
   E. an important objective basis for rating the child

40. Of the following, the one statement that is generally TRUE of the bright pupil is that he

   A. works up to his capacity
   B. is generally better in reading than in mathematics
   C. is more likely to succeed in his social relationships
   D. is likely to be physically superior as well
   E. is quick to form associations between words and ideas

41. Of the following, the MOST important reason why the adolescent period is frequently referred to as a time of conflict, turmoil, and rebellion is that

   A. adolescence is characterized by rapid physiological growth combined with radical changes in body chemistry
   B. adolescents normally meet with frustrations in their efforts to secure financial, personal, and social independence
   C. acne, obesity, skin blemishes, and the attainment of sexual maturity cause hypersensitivity
   D. adolescents experience difficulty in applying previous learnings because their mental and physical resources are drained by their extraordinary physiological changes
   E. the modern program of education has afforded the adolescent new insights into the failures and inadequacies of the *establishment*

42. The MOST important function of the warm-up drill at the beginning of a period is to

A. keep the class busy while the teacher is on hall patrol
B. give the teacher a chance to take attendance
C. provide meaningful drill for skills and concepts previously taught
D. help the teacher get a more accurate mark for each pupil
E. permit the slow learner to catch up with the previous work before the new lesson is begun

43. Of the following, the CHIEF value of the use of audiovisual materials with slow learners is that they   43.___

    A. are attractive and provide entertainment in the learning process
    B. lighten the teacher's load in planning for a lesson
    C. promote conceptual thinking by providing a basis of concrete reality
    D. can teach much more in a given lesson because they minimize the interruptions caused by extraneous pupil questions
    E. can be stopped or held at any point to permit intensive teaching or drill

44. Educational investigations have discovered a strongly positive correlation between a student's academic achievement and   44.___

    A. the small size of his class
    B. the excellence of his attendance
    C. his participation in extra-curricular activities
    D. his motivation
    E. his home environment

45. With regard to a homework assignment, of the following, it is LEAST defensible for it to   45.___

    A. be given in the last minute or two of the lesson
    B. be quite specific
    C. be varied for different class members
    D. involve material covered in previous lessons
    E. require independent research

46. Of the following, the MOST acceptable statement regarding the use of lesson plans in the junior high school is that   46.___

    A. they should not be consulted during the lesson since they distract pupils
    B. they are useful only to new teachers
    C. they require preparation anew each semester even in subject areas that are relatively static
    D. their content should be uniform throughout a school department so that they can be used by substitute teachers
    E. the department should draw up a uniform set of plans for all teachers so that instruction may be equalized for all classes

47. In designing a unit test question of the matching type, the LEAST desirable technique, of the following, would be to   47.___

    A. include two or three more responses than the number of premises
    B. provide at least twenty items in each list to minimize guessing
    C. keep both the premises and responses homogeneous

D. avoid extraneous clues
E. include items that are authentic and relate to the work in hand

48. If a teacher has completed about three-quarters of his lesson and suddenly discovers that there are only three minutes remaining of the period, of the following, the WISEST course of action for him would be to

   A. tell the pupils to refrain from asking questions and make every effort to complete the lesson
   B. select the most important items from the remaining one-quarter of the lesson and summarize them on the board
   C. have the pupils summarize the important ideas that had already been developed in the lesson and, thereafter, revise the next day's lesson plan
   D. complete as much of the lesson as possible and assign the incomplete portion for homework
   E. summarize succinctly for the class the last quarter of the lesson so that the lesson may be fully completed that day

49. In preparing pupils for a uniform examination which all teachers in the department have seen, the BEST procedure, of the following, is for a teacher to

   A. prime pupils on the key questions out of fairness, since other teachers will probably do the same
   B. make up similar questions but in different language and form and drill the class upon them
   C. reveal nothing about the scope or type of questions so that no pupils will have an unfair advantage
   D. give broad hints as to the test questions to slow learners only
   E. indicate to all pupils the scope of the examination and provide practice in questions on the topics covered in the examination

50. A book written by James B. Conant on American education is entitled

   A. THE EDUCATION OF AMERICAN TEACHERS
   B. THE TYRANNY OF TESTING
   C. THE SCHOOLS
   D. THE AMERICAN INTELLECT
   E. IS YOUR CHILD IN THE WRONG GRADE?

## KEY (CORRECT ANSWERS)

| | | | | |
|---|---|---|---|---|
| 1. A | 11. B | 21. A | 31. A | 41. B |
| 2. D | 12. C | 22. A | 32. E | 42. C |
| 3. C | 13. B | 23. E | 33. B | 43. C |
| 4. B | 14. B | 24. B | 34. D | 44. D |
| 5. B | 15. C | 25. D | 35. A | 45. A |
| 6. A | 16. E | 26. C | 36. C | 46. C |
| 7. B | 17. C | 27. E | 37. B | 47. B |
| 8. E | 18. C | 28. A | 38. C | 48. B |
| 9. B | 19. B | 29. C | 39. D | 49. E |
| 10. C | 20. C | 30. D | 40. E | 50. A |

# TEST 2

DIRECTIONS: Each question or incomplete statement is followed by several suggested answers or completions. Select the one that BEST answers the question or completes the statement. *PRINT THE LETTER OF THE CORRECT ANSWER IN THE SPACE AT THE RIGHT.*

1. If the curricular demands of a course of study prevent the teacher from using adequate time to go over the questions on a uniform examination, the BEST procedure of the following would be for him to distribute review questions and       1.____

    A. answer papers and ask pupils to pick out questions for review at random
    B. make an analysis of frequency of errors on those done at home and review the questions most frequently missed first
    C. go over several questions each day over a period of weeks
    D. ask pupils to submit questions about their papers in writing and respond to a few of these each day
    E. model answers, together with scoring keys, which he drew up and used in marking their papers

2. Of the following, the MOST accurate statement regarding oral reports in junior high school classes is that they       2.____

    A. must be carefully supervised for form and content to be effective
    B. are worthwhile chiefly because they provide a change from the monotony of teacher domination
    C. are wasteful of time and provide learning neither for the speaker nor the audience
    D. should be prepared by pupils according to their own dictates to allow for maximum pupil expression
    E. should be extemporaneous and be used, wherever and whenever possible, in place of written reports

3. If a teacher is unsuccessful in eliciting the aim of a lesson through questioning in a few minutes, the MOST acceptable procedure, of the following, would be for the teacher to       3.____

    A. abandon the day's plan and reteach the previous day's work
    B. continue to rephrase pivotal questions to try to elicit the aim for as long as necessary
    C. state the aim and continue with the planned lesson
    D. give a homework assignment designed so as to help elicit the aim the next day
    E. lay this aside and take up the content of the lesson, knowing that the aim will be elicited from the students at an appropriate place in the lesson

4. Of the following, the MOST effective technique for determining whether a written homework assignment is clear is to       4.____

    A. examine in detail each of the assignments turned in the following day
    B. ask the class whether there are any questions about the assignment
    C. review intensively each of the directions in the assignment to make certain that these are understood
    D. have pupils copy the assignment at the beginning of the period to see whether questions arise
    E. discuss the assignment with the class and ask specific questions to test understanding

5. The developmental lesson is LEAST characterized by which one of the following?

   A. Medial and final summaries
   B. Lecture and demonstration
   C. The eliciting of factual information through questioning
   D. The eliciting and clarification of an aim with the help of a motivating technique
   E. The movement of the recitation arrow from pupil → pupil, pupil → teacher, teacher → pupil

6. In distributing questions in a class of pupils of average ability, of the following, it is usually BEST to

   A. start with non-volunteers to develop their interest
   B. ignore non-volunteers
   C. call on volunteers principally until the lesson gains momentum
   D. ask pupils not to volunteer so that each pupil in the class will feel responsible for staying attentive
   E. answer yourself the questions that the volunteers cannot answer

7. Assuming there are three marking periods per term, which one of the following is the BEST approach in arriving at a grade for a student for the second marking period?

   A. Average all test marks of the student for that marking period and assign the multiple of 5 which is closest to this average as his grade.
   B. Average all test marks for each student and assign a grade to a particular student which will indicate his relative standing in the class according to these averages.
   C. Using test marks, class work, and homework as a guide, assign as his grade your estimate of the percentage of the work that has been presented that the student has mastered to date.
   D. Average all test marks of the student since the beginning of the term and assign the multiple of 5 which is closest to this average as his grade.
   E. Averaging test marks, class work, and homework on a weighted basis of 3, 2, and 1, respectively, assign the multiple of 5 which is closest to this average as his grade.

8. The teacher is informed by the parent of one of his pupils that the child will be absent for the next three weeks because of illness.
   Which one of the following is the WISEST course of action for the teacher to follow?

   A. Offer to visit the child frequently during his illness to help him keep up with the class.
   B. Offer to tutor the child privately after he recovers at a nominal fee.
   C. Recommend the services of another teacher who will tutor the child for a fee.
   D. Have one of the children in his class volunteer to visit the sick child each day and transmit the content of the day's lesson and the assignment to him.
   E. Prepare an adequate number of written and study assignments for the child to do during his absence to minimize the effect of the loss of classroom instruction.

9. Which one of the following methods for preventing cheating on tests is MOST effective?   9.____
   A. Mention several methods students use in cheating and warn the class that you will be watching carefully for them.
   B. Prepare two separate tests for alternate rows.
   C. Watch the class carefully and very severely punish the first offender to set an example for the rest.
   D. Call on the services of several Arista members to assist you in proctoring the test.
   E. Directly in front of the class, warn one of the students, whom you suspect to be a ringleader, that you will not tolerate cheating of any kind.

10. A test is considered RELIABLE if it   10.____
    A. measures what it is intended to measure
    B. predicts future behavior
    C. shows consistent growth from previous achievement test scores
    D. measures something consistently
    E. can be counted on to distinguish between the bright, the average, and the slow students

11. Of the following, the one statement that is generally TRUE of the slow learner is that he is   11.____
    A. slow in forming associations between words and ideas
    B. poor in reading but good in arithmetic
    C. more likely to develop into a delinquent
    D. in respect to the general population, at or about the 90th percentile in mechanical ability
    E. more capable of nonverbal reasoning than verbal reasoning

12. In day-to-day practice, the BEST procedure for handling medial summaries of a lesson is that they be   12.____
    A. stated briefly by the teacher
    B. developed into blackboard outlines
    C. elicited from students
    D. be given at the middle of the lesson
    E. developed into mimeographed sheets and be retained in a looseleaf binder

13. Of the following, probably the BEST way for the teacher to determine the true ability of a student is to   13.____
    A. consult frankly with his parents
    B. use a carefully standardized group intelligence test with age-grade equivalents
    C. review his records, observe him very carefully, and analyze his performance
    D. gain the confidence of a physician who has served the family for years
    E. send him to a college psychological testing center and have him take the full complement of tests

14. Of the following, the BEST basis for determining students' grades is usually   14.____
    A. tests *only*
    B. tests, homework, and class participation
    C. tests, homework, class participation, and conduct

D. tests and class participation
E. general estimate, based on their most recent and most successful performances

15. Of the following, the one MOST characteristic of the normally developing adolescent is  15.____

   A. continuous need for parental support
   B. development of emotional maturity
   C. desire for constant domination by siblings
   D. freedom from peer group identification
   E. emphasis on expression of individuality and independence

16. Assuming that a student asks a question which the teacher cannot immediately answer,  16.____
the BEST way, among the following, for the teacher to handle the situation is to

   A. attempt to answer the question anyway
   B. admit he does not know and have the answer looked up and reported to the class at the same or next lesson
   C. state that the question will be answered at a future time
   D. accept the answer of a student who seems to know
   E. ignore the question as though he did not hear it, but then, later on, after finding the answer, refer incidentally to the question and give the answer

17. Of the following, the LEAST effective method for obtaining pupil participation is to  17.____

   A. permit pupils to volunteer to answer
   B. permit pupils to evaluate each others' answers
   C. permit pupils to help develop the wording of the aim of the lesson
   D. use the experiences of pupils in the lesson development
   E. permit pupils to answer in concert

18. Of the following, the record data MOST likely to indicate a slow learner would show that  18.____
the pupil has

   A. repeated failure in mathematics
   B. a mental age considerably higher than the chronological age
   C. reading achievement at the 20th percentile
   D. been an only child of divorced parents
   E. a poor handwriting index

19. Group morale will be higher, as a rule, in classes that are run in which one of the following patterns?  19.____

   A. Democratic      B. Laissez-faire      C. Authoritarian
   D. Individual      E. Pupil-teacher

20. Of the following, the LEAST desirable procedure for the assignment of project work is  20.____
that it should

   A. be requested by the student
   B. provide for teacher conferences with pupils
   C. be given only to superior or gifted students
   D. be a substitute for the daily requirements of the course
   E. take the place of homework

21. The LEAST acceptable of the following procedures for using test scores on teacher-made periodic tests is to

    A. prepare a chart or graph so that each pupil's marks are posted on the bulletin board
    B. train each pupil to keep an individual test score graph in his own notebook
    C. mount only perfect papers on the bulletin board
    D. train each pupil to keep a folder of his own corrected test papers
    E. group children in committees

22. Of the following, the BEST reason for parent-teacher interviews is that the teacher

    A. be enabled to communicate the importance of homework
    B. and the parent share the task of motivating the student
    C. be enabled to advise the parent about the child's needs
    D. be enabled to tell the parent about the child's strength
    E. may be enabled to explain the current philosophy of education, together with principles and practices, of the school

23. A good motivation for a class is always intended to accomplish all of the following EXCEPT

    A. develop a sustained drive
    B. create the feeling of an unsolved problem
    C. communicate the information basic to the lesson to be taught
    D. develop around needs of the adolescent
    E. refer to previous learnings or lessons

24. Which one of the following approaches to the teaching of democratic attitudes is the LEAST effective?

    A. Attitudes should be caught rather than taught.
    B. The learner should identify himself with outstanding democratic leaders.
    C. Direct teaching of moral values will be most productive.
    D. Experiences in democratic living will develop proper democratic attitudes.
    E. Participation in civic affairs shows democracy at work.

25. Which one of the following basic suggestions should one carry out FIRST to establish good class management?

    A. Train the class in distribution of material
    B. Discuss the aims of the year's work
    C. Make out a seating plan
    D. Survey the work of the semester
    E. Discuss the required rules for proper class behavior

26. Of the following, the MOST important element in a problem situation in terms of the pupil's learning is that

    A. the pupil must feel a need or desire to find a solution
    B. the problem situation must come from the experiences of the pupil
    C. there should not be a barrier between the pupil and the solution
    D. the problem should be clear-cut and solvable in only one way
    E. there should be a reward for finding the correct solution

27. Which one of the following is GENERALLY a sound principle of questioning for the teacher to follow?

    A. Speak very loudly to make sure all pupils hear you, especially those who are inattentive.
    B. Repeat pupils' answers to make sure all pupils have heard them.
    C. Distribute questions widely so that all or nearly all pupils have a chance to participate.
    D. Encourage chorus responses so that the teacher will know how many pupils know the answer
    E. Call only upon those who volunteer lest you hurt the feelings of non-volunteers by calling upon them and having them make a spectacle of themselves in front of the whole class

28. A good junior high school lesson will frequently employ which one of the following as its initial phase?

    A. Detailed correction of all parts of the previous night's homework
    B. Explanation of a new kind of problem by the teacher
    C. Warm-up drill for pupils
    D. *Sitting up tall* for extra credit
    E. Good joke with a double entendre

29. Which one of the following descriptions of routines is LEAST indicative of good classroom management?

    A. Initiating distribution of paper by pupil monitor's placing a pile on first desk of each row
    B. Adjusting of windows and shades by a pupil monitor
    C. Placing a sampling of homework examples on chalkboard for correction and discussion
    D. Having students choose seats and then preparing a seating plan for each class
    E. Having a pupil monitor check attendance in your Delaney Book

30. Which one of the following is a CORRECT statement concerning the administration of a pre-test?

    A. It unnecessarily consumes time to acquire information more readily discovered by the teacher by informal means.
    B. It should be confined to the beginning of the school year for the entire grade.
    C. It dispenses with the need for review.
    D. A pre-test is usually given only at the inception of a unit of several weeks' duration.
    E. It serves in part as a survey of individual and class background and readiness.

31. Which one of the following is an INCORRECT procedure in constructing a multiple-choice, short-answer test?

    A. Providing a separate answer sheet, particularly for a long test
    B. Placing a number of easy questions at the beginning of the test
    C. Insuring that correct choices are not obvious
    D. Arranging correct answers according to a pattern
    E. Providing for gradation of difficulty in the sequence of presentation of questions

32. Which one of the following is generally the LEAST effective method of informing pupils of homework assignments?

    A. Dictation of assignments by teacher
    B. Distribution of duplicated assignment sheets
    C. Recording on chalkboard by the teacher before the period begins
    D. Recording on chalkboard by pupil at the beginning of lesson
    E. Making a different student responsible each day for recording the assignment on the chalkboard

33. Of the following, the BEST technique in following up homework is:

    A. The homework should be marked as a test daily
    B. Several students should place their homework on the chalkboard daily
    C. Very little, if any, class time should be consumed in going over homework
    D. Only those exercises and problems with which pupils have difficulty should normally be explained
    E. A monitor in each row should check the homework daily

34. Which one of the following is the LEAST valid method of evaluating a pupil's understanding and readiness for advanced work?

    A. Asking the parent how long the pupil takes to do homework assignments
    B. Observing the pupil as he works on practice material in class
    C. Listening to the pupil's explanation of how he arrived at an answer
    D. Analyzing the pupil's test papers
    E. Examining the pupil's responses as an individual and as a group member

35. When a parent keeps an appointment to visit a teacher to complain about the progress of her child, the teacher may PROPERLY do which one of the following?

    A. Tell the parent that many children in the class are failing.
    B. Ask the parent whether she has carefully supervised her child's homework.
    C. Be fully prepared for the interview by carefully studying the pupil's complete school record.
    D. Point out that the pupil was probably not held to a high standard in previous grades.
    E. Inform the parent that she's lucky that her child has not been kicked out or suspended up to this time.

36. Which one of the following is usually a pedagogically UNSOUND procedure in utilizing a filmstrip with a junior high school class?

    A. Including a follow-up related to the filmstrip in the home study assignment
    B. Employing the filmstrip as a review device
    C. Having pupils read and explain the captions
    D. Showing a complete filmstrip of 47 frames in one period
    E. Asking three or more pithy questions relating the filmstrip to the ongoing unit

37. Of the following possible techniques for use in connection with audio-visual aids, the BEST is for the

    A. students to take notes during the showing of a film
    B. teacher to explain the film during its showing

C. teacher to make auxiliary use of the chalkboard during the showing of the film
D. teacher to stop the film at certain crucial points to emphasize important knowledges or skills
E. class to observe the film without interruption and be questioned about it thereafter

38. Of the following, which one represents the LEAST effective disciplinary technique?  38.___

    A. Compelling pupils under threat of punishment to observe class rules
    B. Helping pupils to enjoy classwork through the use of meaningful activities
    C. Providing wide participation for all pupils in the work and administration of the class
    D. Discouraging lateness to class by starting each period with an interesting activity
    E. Having the homework assignment and/or two or three motivating questions on the board as the class enters the room

39. Which one of the following is a GOOD practical procedure for a teacher to utilize in maintaining discipline?  39.___

    A. Learn the names of all pupils as quickly as possible at the beginning of the year.
    B. Disregard most minor infractions to avoid magnifying their importance.
    C. Prepare a list designating punishments for various infractions and follow it rigidly.
    D. Avoid displaying a sense of humor during the first few weeks of the term.
    E. Maintain a posture of strictness and rigidity for the first third of the term.

40. Of the following, the LEAST desirable technique in performing a demonstration is for the  40.___

    A. teacher to accompany the demonstration with a detailed commentary
    B. apparatus used to be on a large scale
    C. apparatus to be pre-tested
    D. teacher to rehearse the demonstration so that he can perform it easily and smoothly
    E. teacher to have at hand all the apparatus needed for the experiment before he begins his demonstration

41. Of the following, the LEAST desirable technique in performing a demonstration is for the  41.___

    A. teacher to accompany the demonstration with a detailed commentary
    B. apparatus used to be on a large scale
    C. apparatus to be pre-tested
    D. teacher to rehearse the demonstration so that he can perform it easily and smoothly
    E. teacher to have at hand all the apparatus needed for the experiment before he begins his demonstration

42. Learning is MOST apt to happen when the  42.___

    A. pupil understands the importance of what he is doing
    B. pupil is told all the necessary facts by a knowledgeable teacher
    C. pupil handles things
    D. academic standards of the school are kept high
    E. standards of discipline are high and firmly enforced

43. Of the following, the one MOST serious objection to laboratory lessons, as they are usually conducted, is that   43._____

    A. many of the activities are unsafe for unskilled pupils
    B. there is little opportunity for creativity and solving of problems
    C. there is usually insufficient apparatus for individual work by pupils
    D. most of the experiments cannot be performed in a 40-minute laboratory period
    E. they are stereotyped and often on an elementary level, needing little or no demonstration or discovery

44. Whenever possible, a filmstrip should be used rather than a sound motion picture on the same subject because   44._____

    A. it takes less time to show it
    B. it is usually more sequential
    C. it can be used to focus attention more readily where the teacher desires it
    D. the absence of a soundtrack removes a distraction
    E. it is usually better prepared since it deals directly with the topic

45. In order to complete the course of study with a class of slow learners, the teacher should   45._____

    A. skip certain sections which are too difficult
    B. have pupils take copious notes from the blackboard to be studied at home
    C. have pupils read the textbook in class under his direction
    D. plan for varied methods of study of the essential concepts of each unit
    E. make a precis of the remaining work and distribute it in mimeographed form to the students

46. Of the following possible questions for various science lessons, the one which BEST meets the criteria for a good teaching question is:   46._____

    A. Isn't it a fact that the stamen contains the anther?
    B. What about the piston?
    C. What is diastrophism and what theory is used to explain it?
    D. What is the word that denotes a central part or thing about which other parts of things are grouped? It is a six-letter word that begins with *n* and ends with *s*.
    E. Why do glaciers reach beyond the snow line?

47. The MOST important value of a lesson plan book is to   47._____

    A. insure continuity of instruction in the event of the teacher's absence
    B. permit the supervisor to evaluate the quality of work done
    C. enable the teacher to give thought to the work that will be carried on in the class
    D. enable the teacher to dictate important statements
    E. assure that there will be no repetition of work previously covered

48. Reinforcing learning can BEST be achieved when drill is   48._____

    A. given to all pupils regardless of achievement
    B. given in intensive doses
    C. individualized
    D. given without motivation
    E. consistent, continuous, and culminating

49. Thought-provoking answers are MOST easily achieved when

    A. a pupil's name is called before a question is asked
    B. a question is repeated several times in varied forms
    C. a question is asked and then a pupil is called upon to recite
    D. pupils anticipate the question
    E. pupils are advised to think before they speak

50. The teaching effectiveness of class discussions can be improved by all of the following EXCEPT having

    A. pupils face one another in speaking
    B. a competent recorder write main contributions on the blackboard
    C. the brighter pupils offer most of the contributions
    D. the group evaluate its own performance in terms of previously accepted objectives
    E. pupils ask questions of each other and of the teacher

# KEY (CORRECT ANSWERS)

| | | | | |
|---|---|---|---|---|
| 1. B | 11. A | 21. A | 31. D | 41. A |
| 2. A | 12. C | 22. B | 32. A | 42. A |
| 3. C | 13. C | 23. C | 33. D | 43. B |
| 4. E | 14. B | 24. C | 34. A | 44. C |
| 5. B | 15. B | 25. E | 35. C | 45. D |
| 6. C | 16. B | 26. A | 36. D | 46. E |
| 7. C | 17. A | 27. C | 37. E | 47. C |
| 8. E | 18. C | 28. C | 38. A | 48. C |
| 9. B | 19. A | 29. B | 39. A | 49. C |
| 10. D | 20. C | 30. E | 40. B | 50. C |

# EXAMINATION SECTION
# TEST 1

DIRECTIONS: Each question or incomplete statement is followed by several suggested answers or completions. Select the one that BEST answers the question or completes the statement. *PRINT THE LETTER OF THE CORRECT ANSWER IN THE SPACE AT THE RIGHT.*

1. Which one of the following statements about lesson plans is LEAST acceptable? They  1._____
    A. should be done anew each year even if the same subjects are to be taught
    B. should deal with a variety of lesson types and techniques
    C. should include the actual phraseology of pivotal questions to be asked
    D. may be prepared weekly but be flexible enough to permit daily additions and corrections
    E. continue to become less necessary as the teacher's years of experience increase

2. Intervisitation among teachers in a department is GENERALLY  2._____
    A. *unwise,* because teachers should be creative, not imitative
    B. *wise,* because teachers can gain a great deal from sharing methods, procedures, and problems
    C. *unwise,* because teachers do not like to be observed by their colleagues and prefer to be observed, if it is necessary, only by their chairmen
    D. *wise,* because only a few *master teachers* have ideas which are good enough for the others to entertain
    E. *unwise,* because often teachers are affected with an inferiority complex about their own work as they observe superior teachers

3. Which one of the following types of lessons will MOST likely enable a teacher to help children to learn by themselves?  3._____
    A. Supervised study and research
    B. Lecture-demonstration
    C. Developmental
    D. Laboratory-demonstration
    E. Unit

4. Summaries of learnings elicited during and at the end of a lesson are USUALLY  4._____
    A. unproductive, educationally
    B. useful only to slow learners
    C. important in focusing attention on the concepts considered and developed
    D. not so good as summaries dictated by the teacher for copying into the students' notebooks
    E. springboards of motivation for the home assignment

5. Of the following, the generally MOST difficult type of short-answer question is  5._____
    A. multiple choice
    B. completion
    C. true-false
    D. matching
    E. cluster-combination selection

6. When the common element in a number of experiences has been recognized, identified, and employed by a student, then the student has MOST likely formed a(n)    6.___

   A. percept   B. concept   C. objective
   D. principle   E. hypothesis

7. Of the following, the group of persons usually BEST suited to planning and organizing the adaptation of new curricula in a subject area to the needs of a school is    7.___

   A. the principal and his cabinet
   B. the principal and the chairman of the department
   C. the principal, the chairman, and the teachers of the department
   D. a curriculum committee of the division
   E. the principal, the P.T.A., and the vocational advisory board members

8. Of the following possible characteristics of homework assignments, the one which would be MOST likely to distinguish a superior assignment is that it    8.___

   A. provides drill and additional content
   B. enriches and develops the unit under discussion
   C. is uniform for the class but not for the individual student
   D. is thorough and yet very easily checked for completeness
   E. provokes stimulating questions and responses

9. If a class is to be organized into a number of committees to carry on projects to be completed sometime during the term, the BEST of the following arrangements is that each committee consists of    9.___

   A. students of approximately equal ability
   B. at least one student of good ability and the rest of average ability
   C. at least one very good student, one very poor student, and the rest average students
   D. students selected for maximum heterogeneity in respect to range of ability
   E. a proportionate number of students of good ability, average ability, and poor ability

10. Which one of the following possible purposes for which a film might be used in a science class should be considered as of PRIME importance?    10.___

    A. As a means of reviewing a topic
    B. For the viewing of demonstrations that cannot be done readily in the classroom
    C. As a useful change in the normal class routine
    D. To save the teacher's time in the preparation of the required standard demonstrations
    E. As a forceful motivation for the study of the unit

11. Assume that, upon checking the equipment at the end of a laboratory period, and after the class had left the room, a piece of equipment was found missing, and that the teacher is quite certain it was there at the beginning of the period. Which one of the following courses of action should the teacher employ?    11.___

A. Say nothing to the class, and replace the lost equipment as soon as practical
B. Announce the loss to the class the following day, and urge that this equipment be returned quickly and anonymously to a designated area
C. Compel each member of the class to pay an equal share of the cost of replacing the item
D. Deprive the class of laboratory work until the equipment is returned
E. Write a letter to the parents of the students informing them of the situation, and pointing out that the loss of equipment, unless quickly replaced, will seriously retard the education of their children

12. For OPTIMUM preparation, lesson plans should

   A. include all questions to be asked during the lesson and, as a rule, be followed faithfully
   B. contain only the pivotal questions, and permit a certain amount of flexibility
   C. cover an entire unit's work regardless of the number of days it lasts
   D. be the same for all classes of the same grade of work
   E. be of uniform length and structure, covering no more than one-fifth of a unit in any one lesson

13. Of the following, the MOST significant outcome of a laboratory lesson is that it

   A. emphasizes the scientific method
   B. demonstrates to pupils how to solve problems of a scientific nature
   C. teaches the pupil skills that he will need in college
   D. leads to significant outcomes in self-direction and self-learning
   E. gives the pupil first-hand experience with the concepts studied

14. Which one of the following statements expresses the LEAST valid purpose of a demonstration for a lesson in science? To

   A. evoke a problem that the class can solve through activity and discussion
   B. furnish information that cannot be found in the text
   C. save time because the class has fallen behind in its coverage of content
   D. provide a motivation for a subsequent laboratory lesson
   E. test certain hypotheses or to check results

15. The readiness of a class to begin a new unit of study can BEST be ascertained by

   A. asking the students to raise their hands if they feel ready to proceed to the new unit
   B. testing the class on the knowledges and skills necessary as the foundation for the new unit
   C. showing an appropriate film and asking for reactions to it
   D. organizing several teachers into a team which will observe and judge the readiness of the classes concerned
   E. evaluating the results of a test on the preceding unit

16. The activity of a science class in a laboratory should USUALLY be halted

   A. several times during the period to make sure that all pupils are progressing at the same rate
   B. about 9 minutes before the end of the period in order to insure adequate clean-up time and make possible a brief summary of the learnings

C. about 16-21 minutes before the end of the period in order to insure adequate clean-up time and make possible a full discussion of the learnings
D. at the dismissal bell in order to insure maximum work time
E. once at the beginning of the period and once at the end to ensure proper adherence to rules of safety

17. Of the following, probably the GREATEST fault in lecturing as a method of teaching is the    17.___

    A. tendency to associate demonstrations with the lecture
    B. substitution of audio-visual aids for part of the lecture
    C. lack of student activity and participation
    D. tendency of a good lecturer to be a good actor
    E. great variation in this ability among the teaching staff

18. A pedagogical problem arising in a high school classroom which cannot be solved by the teacher should, in general, properly be referred FIRST to the    18.___

    A. director of the subject area
    B. superintendent in charge of instruction
    C. chairman of the department
    D. author of the textbook
    E. vice principal in charge of instruction

19. An educationally sound film on a new unit should generally be shown    19.___

    A. at the inception of the unit
    B. after the unit has been partially developed in classroom activities
    C. as the culminating activity in the unit
    D. as an extra-curricular activity
    E. at any time that interest in the unit appears to be lagging

20. Of the following, the MOST significant criticism of the lecture method is that it fails adequately to    20.___

    A. develop content and present concepts
    B. stimulate scientific research
    C. meet adolescents' social and personal needs
    D. develop self-discipline and self-interest
    E. involve teacher participation and preparation

21. When 45 test papers are ranked from high to low, the score of the 23rd paper is ALWAYS called the    21.___

    A. mode                              B. standard score
    C. standard error of deviation       D. median score
    E. semiquartile deviation

22. The degree to which a test measures what it is supposed to measure is called its    22.___

    A. reliability      B. consistency      C. objectivity
    D. validity         E. authenticity

23. Of the following, an educational approach to teaching which is being employed on a large scale at this time is one  23._____

    A. employing a veteran teacher and assistant teachers with a large group of pupils
    B. recommending abandonment of all pupil laboratory experimentation
    C. advocating the use of television as the major means of learning
    D. suggesting the elimination of practically all textbooks in the teaching process
    E. involving the substitution of college education majors for teachers

24. Which one of the following is distinctly NOT the responsibility of the homeroom teacher?  24._____

    A. Encourage overage students who are doing poorly in school to drop out of school and go to work
    B. Discuss with students the possible courses they may request for next term
    C. Assist students to get help in handling homework difficulties in various subjects
    D. Encourage students to join school clubs and organizations which will meet their needs
    E. Teach formal guidance lessons on various topics

25. Of the following possible justifications for surprise quizzes, the BEST one is that  25._____

    A. they are periodically necessary to deflate the sense of superiority of the students who regularly get high marks
    B. it is a good way to punish a class for poor discipline with these quizzes
    C. they motivate the students to study regularly
    D. they cause the students to have more respect for the ability of the teacher
    E. they serve to concretize and to highlight the important learnings to be acquired

# KEY (CORRECT ANSWERS)

| | | | | |
|---|---|---|---|---|
| 1. | E | | 11. | B |
| 2. | B | | 12. | B |
| 3. | A | | 13. | E |
| 4. | C | | 14. | C |
| 5. | B | | 15. | B |
| 6. | B | | 16. | B |
| 7. | C | | 17. | C |
| 8. | B | | 18. | C |
| 9. | D | | 19. | B |
| 10. | B | | 20. | C |

21. D
22. D
23. A
24. A
25. C

# TEST 2

DIRECTIONS: Each question or incomplete statement is followed by several suggested answers or completions. Select the one that BEST answers the question or completes the statement. *PRINT THE LETTER OF THE CORRECT ANSWER IN THE SPACE AT THE RIGHT.*

1. Which one of the following statements BEST describes the purposes of questioning?  1.___

    A. Questions should be challenging, arouse attention, stimulate thinking, and encourage good expression in the answers given.
    B. Simple factual questions should be asked often to serve as the teacher's best evaluative device.
    C. Questions should be repeated to make sure that every student understands them.
    D. Multiple questions should be asked occasionally to encourage clear thinking in complex situations.
    E. At times, the whip-lash type of question should be used in getting slow learners to respond.

2. Of the following, the one which may BEST be achieved through a system of programmed instruction is:  2.___

    A. Allowing a student to proceed at his own pace
    B. Reducing the number of teaching positions
    C. Providing study materials for homebound students
    D. Providing practice materials for students of low mental and/or reading ability
    E. Completing coverage of the course of study

3. To clarify course objectives and daily aims for the students, the BEST procedure is for these objectives and aims to be  3.___

    A. clearly stated by the teacher
    B. raised by the students, discussed, and accepted by them
    C. written on the blackboard before they are discussed
    D. written on the blackboard after explanation by the teacher and then copied into notebooks by the students
    E. elicited from the faculty and the P.T.A. and transmitted to the students

4. Which one of the following methods for getting a lesson started promptly is LEAST sound pedagogically?  4.___

    A. Have a challenging motivating question on the blackboard at the beginning of the period
    B. Stand near the door with the marking book and give a zero to any student who does not sit down and take out his work at once
    C. Give a quiz on the previous lesson at the beginning of the period
    D. Stand quietly, yet firmly, in front of the room and wait for attention
    E. Refer to a current event or happening at the start of the class

5. Of the following, experience with various kinds of tests and measurements utilized for predicting the academic success of pupils in advanced high school courses and honor classes in a given subject has shown *particularly* that  5.___

A. an aptitude test is the most satisfactory single instrument
B. previous achievement represented by pupil's grades in that subject is the most accurate yardstick
C. all other factors should be subordinated to the I.Q. and the M.A.
D. the child's motivation is the decisive factor
E. teachers' estimates and evaluations bear great weight

6. It has been found that *learning by wholes,* i.e., being challenged by a total situation, is generally MOST readily effected by which one of the following groups?

   A. Dull-normal pupils in the tenth year
   B. Girls in the senior year
   C. Pupils whose attention span is small but whose interest span is large
   D. Pupils in special education classes in the ninth and tenth years
   E. The superior pupils of whatever school year

7. Which one of the following questions asked by a teacher is MOST acceptable?

   A. The answer to Question 5 is what?
   B. Mary, is her answer to Question 5 right?
   C. What is your answer to Question 5, George?
   D. Class, tell George the answer to Question 5.
   E. George, what is your answer to Question 5?

8. The technique of using a team-teaching design which includes a master teacher, regular teachers, and teacher-aides is based MOST directly upon which one of the following concepts?

   A. Teachers who have served faithfully deserve master teacher status.
   B. An unparalleled opportunity is provided for teacher training of large numbers of teachers and beginning teachers.
   C. The conservation of public funds is a moral obligation.
   D. Teacher-aides are often more knowledgeable and skillful than teachers.
   E. Teaching is a complex art requiring different levels of competence and training.

9. In THE AMERICAN HIGH SCHOOL TODAY, James B. Conant proposed that

   A. the four-year high school should be a comprehensive high school
   B. the present curriculum in the fourth year of high school is more appropriate for a *community junior college*
   C. *social living* courses should be added in all high schools to provide better life adjustment in our atomic era
   D. standardized achievement tests have outlived their usefulness
   E. a national intelligence test be given to all students at stated intervals

10. The validity of intelligence tests as instruments for evaluating native ability has been questioned because these tests tend to

    A. lack reliability, especially for gifted children
    B. lack reliability, especially for pupils of low motor coordination who consequently have a poor sense of spatial relations
    C. place too much emphasis on mathematical and scientific aptitude
    D. stress verbal, as opposed to non-verbal, elements of intelligence
    E. have an experiential base which is foreign to culturally different children in poverty areas

11. Of the following, the MAJOR aim for giving a standardized test to classes at the beginning of a new course is *probably* to

    A. discover weaknesses of previous teaching
    B. discover interests, aptitudes, and previous learnings in this area
    C. give teachers and supervisors a basis for deciding upon the regrouping of classes in terms of ability
    D. arouse pupil curiosity and provide a base for motivation
    E. give students and teachers a definite basis for class rankings

12. Of the following terms, the one MOST closely associated with the sum-total of response patterns and abilities possessed by the learner at any given time is

    A. adaptation        B. readiness        C. reinforcement
    D. response          E. motivation

13. Which one of the following sets of statements BEST explains the occurrence of disciplinary infractions among adolescents in secondary schools?

    A. Adolescents tend to resist authority; they seek the admiration of their peers; they are not convinced that poor self-control is necessarily harmful to future success.
    B. Syllabi are teacher-imposed; rules of conduct in secondary schools are unrealistic.
    C. Adolescents undergo rapid physical growth; their span of attention is short; they are incapable of abstract thoughts.
    D. Adolescence has been extended by modern society; rules of conduct do not parallel chronological age; there is a widespread lack of pre-vocational meaningful study.
    E. The violence and excesses of World War II have led to a continuing decline, on the part of all classes and groups, in respect to the acceptance of the authority symbol; this defiance does not even stop at anarchy; it presages a complete breakdown of responsible democratic government, as we have known it.

14. Of the following, the MAIN reason why psychologists warn against over-emphasis of rewards-and-punishment motivation in teaching is that this type of motivation

    A. ignores the more effective stimulus of inner satisfaction
    B. inevitably leads to a listless class atmosphere
    C. has little or no influence with the bright child
    D. often leads by easy stages to corporal punishment
    E. is artificial and has but a temporary effect

15. Pragmatism as an educational philosophy was stressed by

    A. Dewey         B. Terman        C. Binet
    D. Pestalozzi    E. Cubberley

16. A boy has scored 57% on a test in a modified (slow) class. Which one of the following comments by the teacher is MOST likely to stimulate him towards sustained scholastic improvement?

A. Why didn't you study harder?
B. Some of your answers showed very good understanding.
C. You will have to work much harder to get out of the slow class.
D. I had hoped that you would prove that we had been wrong in putting you into the slow class.
E. I know that you're not that much of a drop. You should do better next time.

17. Which one of the following statements concerning the aim of a lesson is MOST valid?    17.____

    A. The teacher should write the aim on the blackboard at the beginning of each lesson.
    B. The aim should be an outgrowth of, and developed from, the motivation.
    C. Each child should write the aim of each lesson in his notebook each day.
    D. The teacher should announce the aim of the lesson to the class at the beginning of each period.
    E. Students should be called on, one by one, to state
    F. the aim of the lesson until common agreement is reached.

18. The MOST important value of a teacher's lesson plan is to    18.____

    A. enable the chairman to determine whether the teacher is to follow the syllabus
    B. enable the teacher to evaluate the teaching he has done
    C. ensure continuity of instruction in the event of the teacher's absence
    D. provide an opportunity for the teacher to give organized thought to work that will be carried on by the class
    E. provide for the many varied abilities and interests present in the classroom

19. Which one of the following is usually MOST basic in determining the effectiveness of a given lesson having an appropriate aim? The    19.____

    A. logical organization of the subject matter
    B. adequacy of the teacher's presentation of the aim of the lesson
    C. absence of classroom misbehavior on the part of the pupils
    D. relationship of the lesson to the felt needs and interests of the teacher
    E. degree of pupil involvement in the learning activity

20. Of the following, probably the BEST method for a teacher to use in helping students retain the material learned in class is to    20.____

    A. insist on note-taking
    B. encourage memorization
    C. use and re-use the material in various meaningful situations
    D. encourage cramming for quizzes
    E. give frequent tests which cover *back* material as well as the present unit

21. The *stimulus-response* aspects of programmed instruction are MOST closely associated with the precepts advanced by which one of the following authors?    21.____

    A. James Conant           B. Skinner
    C. Martin Mayer           D. Jacques Barzun
    E. John Kenneth Galbraith

22. Among the following types of tests, the one MOST difficult to evaluate objectively is	22.___

   A. multiple choice	B. completion
   C. true-false	D. modified true-false
   E. matching

23. Of the following functions of tests, the one that is LEAST defensible *pedagogically* is	23.___

   A. guidance and class placement
   B. assignment of report card marks
   C. diagnosis of specific weaknesses
   D. stimulus to do homework
   E. record of achievement

24. Which one of the following is TRUE of a *normal* distribution of test scores?	24.___

   A. More scores fall below the average than above.
   B. More scores fall above the average than below.
   C. Scores become progressively less frequent as they deviate further from the average.
   D. Scores tend to extend further above the average than below.
   E. There is no *normal* distribution of test scores in actual fact, no matter what the extent of sampling.

25. When a student answers a question so that most of the class cannot hear him, the LEAST effective of the following practices is for the teacher to	25.___

   A. repeat the answer
   B. require the student to stand and face the class
   C. ask another student to repeat the answer
   D. have the student repeat his answer
   E. ask the class how many heard him

## KEY (CORRECT ANSWERS)

| | | | |
|---|---|---|---|
| 1. | A | 11. | B |
| 2. | A | 12. | B |
| 3. | B | 13. | A |
| 4. | B | 14. | A |
| 5. | B | 15. | A |
| 6. | E | 16. | B |
| 7. | C | 17. | B |
| 8. | E | 18. | D |
| 9. | A | 19. | E |
| 10. | E | 20. | C |

21. B
22. B
23. D
24. C
25. A

# TEST 3

DIRECTIONS: Each question or incomplete statement is followed by several suggested answers or completions. Select the one that BEST answers the question or completes the statement. *PRINT THE LETTER OF THE CORRECT ANSWER IN THE SPACE AT THE RIGHT.*

1. Of the following, it is NOT a good characteristic for a question to 1.___

    A. be simply stated
    B. be clear in meaning
    C. be part of a logical sequence
    D. to give no clue to the answer
    E. require a simple yes or no answer

2. Which one of the following is MOST desirable for the teacher to do in assigning homework? 2.___

    A. Read the assignment orally at the beginning of the lesson.
    B. Assign only questions that all pupils can answer.
    C. Base a portion of such assignments upon the textbook questions.
    D. Spend some class time in clarifying the assignment.
    E. Insist that the assignment be executed in full-sentenced continuous discourse.

3. Gestalt psychologists state as one of their more important concepts that learning takes place MOST effectively when the material 3.___

    A. is rehearsed mentally as often as possible
    B. is put into a meaningful context
    C. does not elicit interfering, repressing associations
    D. is associated with something pleasant
    E. relates to the needs and interests of the community

4. The PRIMARY objective of guidance is to promote which one of the following in students? 4.___

    A. Increased capacity for self-direction
    B. Mastery of subject matter
    C. Maximum achievement within the limits of their capacity
    D. Need to conform to school regulations
    E. Awareness of the world around them

5. Of the following, which one is usually LEAST effective as a means of dealing with individual differences in the classroom? 5.___

    A. Heterogeneous grouping
    B. The lecture method
    C. Differential assignments
    D. The *unit* method of teaching-learning organization
    E. Committee assignments and reports

6. A PRIMARY purpose of homogeneous grouping is to 6.___

    A. cut down class size
    B. prevent conflict between ethnic groups

C. decrease the teacher's work
D. enable a maximum number of students to achieve optimally
E. simplify pupil personnel accounting

7. Of the following, the one which represents an ADVANTAGE of the demonstration method in science teaching over the laboratory approach is that it

    A. can stimulate pupil interest to a higher degree
    B. establishes principles of science more firmly
    C. affords an economy of apparatus and materials
    D. more effectively encourages pupils to use scientific methods
    E. emphasizes concepts over facts

7._____

8. Which one of the following is the LEAST important factor in a successful laboratory lesson in science?

    A. The influence of the teacher
    B. The regular use of carefully developed fill-in laboratory manuals
    C. Having all pupils participate actively in the laboratory
    D. Providing for many resources for experimentation
    E. Careful planning and preparation by the teacher and students

8._____

9. Of the following, the one which would BEST provide for effective, creative teaching is

    A. emphasizing student memorization of the important sets of facts
    B. following a carefully developed uniform methodology to improve efficiency of teaching and learning
    C. permitting students to decide all important classroom management problems in order to encourage initiative
    D. leading students to feel the need for learning the various topics in the course of study
    E. affording maximum opportunity for disagreement and alternatives in the classroom

9._____

10. Of the following, the LEAST likely topic for which home economics and science teachers should cooperate in providing common pupil experiences is

    A. nutrition
    B. refrigeration
    C. atomic structure
    D. home appliances
    E. strength of materials

10._____

11. Of the following criteria for determining the quality of a classroom discussion, the one which is LEAST important is whether or not it

    A. serves to identify and refine the problem under discussion
    B. provides for a useful exchange of ideas
    C. consists of a series of questions and answers
    D. helps to interpret information and draw conclusions
    E. produces meaningful effects on the content, objectives, materials, methods, and evaluation of instruction

11._____

12. The MOST desirable type of classroom discipline is BEST attained through which one of the following practices?

    A. Encouraging traits of self-discipline
    B. Including class behavior in the final rating
    C. Establishing the idea that rules and regulations will be strictly enforced
    D. Anticipating difficulty and sending the first few minor cases of breach of discipline to the chairman or dean
    E. Maintaining a permissive or a restrictive atmosphere in the classroom but never a mixture of both

13. A test may be said to be reliable when

    A. it consistently measures what it purports to measure
    B. it adequately deals with the types of educational outcomes to be measured at proper levels of difficulty for pupils
    C. there is a high correlation between test scores and criteria measures
    D. it can be obtained on time from publishers
    E. it measures accurately whatever it does measure

14. Of the following, the one which does NOT measure the concentration of scores in any set of scores or group of data is the

    A. mode   B. modulus   C. mean   D. median   E. middle

15. Of the following, the GREATEST advantage of short-answer tests is the

    A. ease with which the test items can be constructed
    B. ease with which such tests can be standardized
    C. wide sampling of the subject matter of the course
    D. ease with which the test results can be interpreted
    E. large number of questions that can be given as contrasted with the essay test

16. The MAIN advantage of standardized tests is

    A. objectivity
    B. ease of marking for teachers
    C. marks may be compared with other groups
    D. that they provide greater motivation for students
    E. they are held *secure*

17. A percentile score of 55 is

    A. a score equivalent to the arithmetic mean of the scores
    B. equaled or exceeded by 45% of the scores in the distribution
    C. equivalent to a score of 55 out of 100
    D. the accepted norm
    E. equivalent to a raw score of 55

18. The process of reviewing homework daily is time-consuming. Of the following suggestions made by a group of teachers, which one is MOST sound pedagogically?

    A. Do not go over the homework at all
    B. Go over, in class, only the problems with which pupils had trouble

C. Collect the homework of only one row at a time and return it corrected the next day
D. Collect the homework of the whole class once a week on a specific day
E. Before going on to the new lesson, be sure to go over all the homework

19. Which one of the following is the BEST statement about a teacher's technique of questioning?

    A. No question should be so difficult that even the slowest pupil couldn't answer it.
    B. Each lesson should have at least one question which would require the pupils to do critical thinking.
    C. There should be a series of pivotal questions to highlight the chief learnings.
    D. Each question should be simple and short
    E. At times, use the *whip-lash* or *tugging* types with slow learners.

20. Of the following, the BEST statement concerning skill in questioning is:

    A. To make sure all students hear, the teacher should often repeat her question
    B. Answers should be repeated because some children sit far away from the pupil who is answering
    C. Each question should be addressed to a particular pupil by giving his name before asking the question
    D. To vary the kinds of questions, include the double question, particularly for bright students
    E. A question should be addressed to the entire class

21. Of the following, the LEAST effective method for obtaining pupil participation is to

    A. give a warm-up drill to the entire class
    B. group the class and give different assignments to each group
    C. have pupils answer in concert
    D. use experiences of pupils in the lesson development
    E. ask thought-provoking pivotal questions

22. A test which is too difficult will USUALLY yield scores that fall into a _____ distribution.

    A. bell-shaped          B. negatively skewed
    C. positively skewed    D. bimodal
    E. variety of patterns of

23. The MOST desirable routine procedure for going over homework is to

    A. compare answers orally with the class
    B. have students put their work on the board and explain it to the rest of the class
    C. have the teacher do each example together with the class
    D. collect it and mark it outside of class, returning it within a week
    E. ask students to raise their hands if they have the correct answer as it is announced by the teacher

24. Of the following characteristics of a good lesson plan, the one which applies LEAST is that it

    A. forms part of a larger unit
    B. helps give direction to the lesson
    C. be adhered to even if vital side issues appear
    D. focuses on a meaningful problem
    E. refers to previous lessons and learnings

25. The degree to which a test is stable and trustworthy is called its

    A. validity
    B. coefficient of correlation
    C. objectivity
    D. reliability
    E. consistency

## KEY (CORRECT ANSWERS)

| | | | |
|---|---|---|---|
| 1. | E | 11. | C |
| 2. | D | 12. | A |
| 3. | B | 13. | E |
| 4. | A | 14. | B |
| 5. | B | 15. | C |
| 6. | D | 16. | C |
| 7. | C | 17. | B |
| 8. | B | 18. | B |
| 9. | D | 19. | C |
| 10. | C | 20. | E |

| | |
|---|---|
| 21. | C |
| 22. | C |
| 23. | B |
| 24. | C |
| 25. | D |

# TEST 4

DIRECTIONS: Each question or incomplete statement is followed by several suggested answers or completions. Select the one that BEST answers the question or completes the statement. *PRINT THE LETTER OF THE CORRECT ANSWER IN THE SPACE AT THE RIGHT.*

1. Of the following audio-visual aids, the one that represents the MOST recent innovation in science teaching is 1.____

    A. single topic films
    B. filmstrips
    C. 2x2-inch colored slides
    D. 16-mm sound films
    E. 8-mm sound films

2. Of the following reasons for using charts as a teaching device in the classroom, the MOST desirable one is the 2.____

    A. ease with which large numbers of charts can be stored
    B. ability to use color for both functional and decorative effect
    C. ability to include many details about a topic on one chart
    D. ability to make comparisons between various things, places, distances, conditions, etc.
    E. ease with which they can be followed in a class discussion

3. Of the following reasons for including essay questions in an examination, the one that is probably MOST important is that this type of question 3.____

    A. provides greater coverage of material than other test items
    B. is easier to formulate than good objective-type questions
    C. provides opportunities for subjective evaluation of answers
    D. provides for pupil expression in an organized manner and in depth
    E. emphasizes thinking through rather than mere recall

4. Of the following practices for helping a beginning teacher in the classroom, the BEST would probably be to 4.____

    A. have informal discussions with colleagues at opportune times
    B. continue taking courses at the local colleges
    C. follow a planned program of intervisitation
    D. attend departmental conferences devoted to pedagogy
    E. ask the principal or chairman to sit in on his first month of teaching

5. Of the following reasons for using, at times, a single loop movie projector rather than a 16-mm movie projector, the one reason that is INCORRECT is that it(s) 5.____

    A. is faster to load and unload film
    B. can be used in a more flexible manner
    C. can be used without darkening the room
    D. soundtrack can produce sound of functional fidelity
    E. soundtrack can produce sound of higher fidelity

6. Of the following reasons for experimenting with team teaching methods, the one that is probably MOST valid from an educational point of view is that it 6.____

75

A. sawould help meet the problem of teacher shortage
B. would provide overburdened teachers with more free time
C. makes provision for flexible scheduling and independent study by pupils
D. can easily be incorporated into old as well as new school plans
E. would provide more highly skilled teachers

7. In considering the roles of a homeroom teacher, the one of the following which would probably be considered LEAST important from an educational viewpoint is to

A. give guidance, since the school has licensed guidance counselors
B. keep accurate and up-to-date school records for students
C. provide a program of tutorial assistance for students that need help
D. maintain firm discipline while routine school matters are being handled
E. establish liaison with the parents of the students

8. Of the following practices followed by teachers in doing project work, the one that probably has the LEAST merit is to

A. require that every student submit an individual project
B. display class projects in a science fair held in the school
C. encourage students to work in committees on group projects
D. provide opportunity for pupils to discuss their work on school time
E. organize a project center where displays of the best work may be seen

9. Of the following types of objective questions, the one that is considered MOST flexible and statistically reliable is the

A. modified true-false
B. matching
C. completion
D. multiple choice
E. true-false

10. Of the following, probably the LEAST valuable way to begin a new topic or lesson is for the teacher to

A. distribute a step-by-step outline of the topics or lesson
B. explore some interest already possessed by the student
C. elicit an explanation of the importance of the subject
D. develop an overview of the subject
E. refer to some current event

11. In administering the Iowa Tests of Educational Development, the one factor among the following that is NOT a primary aim is to

A. identify the intellectually gifted
B. show parents the fixed limitations of their children
C. serve as backgrounds for conferences between parents and counselors
D. select students for remedial classes
E. aid in ability grouping

12. Of the following, the one statement that is generally TRUE of the bright pupil is that he

A. works up to his capacity
B. is generally better in reading than in mathematics
C. is more likely to succeed in his social relationships

D. is likely to be physically superior as well
E. is quick to form associations between words and ideas

13. Of the following, the MOST important reason why the adolescent period is frequently referred to as a time of conflict, turmoil, and rebellion is that

   A. adolescence is characterized by rapid physiological growth combined with radical changes in body chemistry
   B. adolescents normally meet with frustrations in their efforts to secure financial, personal, and social independence
   C. acne, obesity, skin blemishes, and the attainment of sexual maturity cause hypersensitivity
   D. adolescents experience difficulty in applying previous learnings because their mental and physical resources are drained by their extraordinary physiological changes
   E. the modern program of education has afforded the adolescent new insights into the failures and inadequacies of the *establishment*

14. The MOST important function of the warm-up drill at the beginning of a period is to

   A. keep the class busy while the teacher is on hall patrol
   B. give the teacher a chance to take attendance
   C. provide meaningful drill for skills and concepts previously taught
   D. help the teacher get a more accurate mark for each pupil
   E. permit the slow learner to catch up with the previous work before the new lesson is begun

15. Of the following, the CHIEF value of the use of audiovisual materials with slow learners is that they

   A. are attractive and provide entertainment in the learning process
   B. lighten the teacher's load in planning for a lesson
   C. promote conceptual thinking by providing a basis of concrete reality
   D. can teach much more in a given lesson because they minimize the interruptions caused by extraneous pupil questions
   E. can be stopped or held at any point to permit intensive teaching or drills

16. Educational investigations have discovered a strongly positive correlation between a student's academic achievement and

   A. the small size of his class
   B. the excellence of his attendance
   C. his participation in extra-curricular activities
   D. his motivation
   E. his home environment

17. With regard to a homework assignment, of the following, it is LEAST defensible for it to

   A. be given in the last minute or two of the lesson
   B. be quite specific
   C. be varied for different class members
   D. involve material covered in previous lessons
   E. require independent research

18. Of the following, the MOST acceptable statement regarding the use of lesson plans in the junior high school is that

   A. they should not be consulted during the lesson since they distract pupils
   B. they are useful only to new teachers
   C. they require preparation anew each semester even in subject areas that are relatively static
   D. their content should be uniform throughout a school department so that they can be used by substitute teachers
   E. the department should draw up a uniform set of plans for all teachers so that instruction may be equalized for all classes

19. In designing a unit-test question of the matching type, the LEAST desirable technique, of the following, would be to

   A. include two or three more responses than the number of premises
   B. provide at least twenty items in each list to minimize guessing
   C. keep both the premises and responses homogeneous
   D. avoid extraneous clues
   E. include items that are authentic and relate to the work in hand

20. If a teacher has completed about three-quarters of his lesson and suddenly discovers that there are only three minutes remaining in the period, of the following, the WISEST course of action for him would be to

   A. tell the pupils to refrain from asking questions and make every effort to complete the lesson
   B. select the most important items from the remaining one-quarter of the lesson and summarize them on the board
   C. have the pupils summarize the important ideas that have already been developed in the lesson and, thereafter, revise the next day's lesson plan
   D. complete as much of the lesson as possible and resume the lesson the following day
   E. summarize succinctly for the class the last quarter of the lesson so that the lesson may be fully completed that day

21. In preparing pupils for a uniform examination which all teachers in the department have seen, the BEST procedure, of the following, is for a teacher to

   A. prime pupils on the key questions out of fairness since other teachers will probably do the same
   B. make up similar questions but in different language and form and drill the class upon them
   C. reveal nothing about the scope or type of questions so that no pupil will have an unfair advantage
   D. give broad hints as to the test questions to slow learners only
   E. indicate to all pupils the scope of the examination and provide practice in questions on the topics covered in the examination

22. If the curricular demands of a course of study prevent the teacher from using adequate time to go over the questions on a uniform examination, the BEST procedure, of the following, would be for him to distribute review questions and   22.____

    A. answer papers and ask pupils to pick out questions for review at random
    B. make an analysis of frequency of errors on those done at home and review the questions most frequently missed first
    C. go over several questions each day over a period of weeks
    D. ask pupils to submit questions about their papers in writing and respond to a few of these each day
    E. model answers, together with scoring keys, which he drew up and used in marking their papers

23. Of the following, the MOST accurate statement regarding oral reports in junior high school classes is that they   23.____

    A. must be carefully supervised for form and content to be effective
    B. are worthwhile chiefly because they provide a change from the monotony of teacher domination
    C. are wasteful of time and provide learning neither for the speaker nor the audience
    D. should be prepared by pupils according to their own dictates to allow for maximum pupil expression
    E. should be extemporaneous and be used, wherever and whenever possible, in place of written reports

24. If a teacher is unsuccessful in eliciting the aim of a lesson through questioning in a few minutes, the MOST acceptable procedure, of the following, would be for the teacher to   24.____

    A. abandon the day's plan and reteach the previous day's work
    B. continue to rephrase pivotal questions to try to elicit the aim for as long as necessary
    C. state the aim and continue with the planned lesson
    D. give a homework assignment designed so as to help elicit the aim the next day
    E. lay this aside and take up the content of the lesson, knowing that the aim will be elicited from the students at an appropriate place in the lesson

25. The developmental lesson is LEAST characterized by which one of the following?   25.____

    A. Medial and final summaries
    B. Lecture and demonstration
    C. The eliciting of factual information through questioning
    D. The eliciting and clarification of an aim with the help of a motivating technique
    E. The movement of the recitation arrow from pupil → pupil, pupil → teacher, teacher → pupil

## KEY (CORRECT ANSWERS)

1. A
2. E
3. D
4. C
5. E

6. C
7. D
8. A
9. D
10. A

11. B
12. E
13. B
14. C
15. C

16. D
17. A
18. C
19. B
20. D

21. E
22. B
23. A
24. C
25. B

# EXAMINATION SECTION
## TEST 1

DIRECTIONS: Each question or incomplete statement is followed by several suggested answers or completions. Select the one that BEST answers the question or completes the statement. *PRINT THE LETTER OF THE CORRECT ANSWER IN THE SPACE AT THE RIGHT.*

1. The statement among the following which is NOT appropriately applied to the modern concept of individualized education is:

    A. Growth and learning are almost synonymous.
    B. Readiness for learning is determined by the individual's intellectual acumen.
    C. Standardized teaching methods may run counter to the individual's optimum learning methods.
    D. The good life is not fully realized unless maximum individual and social growth is taking place.

2. The description among the following which is NOT properly associated with core curriculum is:

    A. Units which cut across subject fields and which may be taught by one or more teachers are used.
    B. Learning is centered on large topics around which activities are organized.
    C. Pupils play a major part in planning, launching, and developing the work of the group.
    D. Activities, excursions, and community resources are utilized instead of textbooks and research.

3. In which one of the following areas does conditioning play a major role?

    A. Development of motor skills
    B. Acquisition of facts
    C. Development of attitudes
    D. Formation of concepts

4. Most present-day psychologists accept the principle that drill should be used in the modern classroom only when

    A. reviewing material that has already been covered
    B. it is necessary to clarify pupil understanding of a concept
    C. test results reveal poor mastery of factual material
    D. an automatic response is considered desirable

5. Of the following, which would ordinarily be the LEAST effective means of modifying an attitude?

    A. Listening to a lecture
    B. Role playing
    C. A panel discussion following a film
    D. Group discussion

6. In the guidance of pupil learning, research has indicated that 6.___

   A. emphasis on correct responses is more effective than emphasis on errors
   B. demonstration is more effective than practice
   C. massed practice is more effective than distributed practice
   D. verbal guidance is more effective than demonstration

7. In grades kindergarten through 2, mathematics is taught by the teacher 7.___

   A. in a definite sequence, beginning in first grade
   B. in a definite sequence, beginning in the kindergarten
   C. in a definite sequence, beginning in the second grade
   D. as the topics arise naturally from projects in other areas or from real experiences

8. Which one of the following procedures is of MOST value in developing problem-solving ability in grades 1-4? 8.___

   A. Children should be encouraged to solve problems in a variety of ways.
   B. Children should represent problems symbolically before attempting to solve them.
   C. Most problems should be presented to children in written form.
   D. Problems presented in written form should be discussed before children attempt to solve them.

9. Which one of the following incentives should be stressed by the teacher in promoting learning of a given skill by her pupils? 9.___

   A. Need to use the skill
   B. Desire to please the teacher
   C. Fear of low grades or failure
   D. Desire for good grades

10. The rate of forgetting of information acquired by rote memorization is 10.___

    A. gradually accelerating
    B. gradually decelerating
    C. slow at first, and then more rapid
    D. rapid at first, and then slower

11. Questioning is one of the most valuable devices of the teacher. Of the following, which statement is the LEAST valid? 11.___

    A. A good question provides for reflective or critical thinking.
    B. Teachers' questions can directly affect the development of children's thinking skills.
    C. Questions are useful in diagnosing an individual child's progress.
    D. Effective questions result from the innate talents of teachers.

12. Each of the following principles is valid in daily planning EXCEPT that it 12.___

    A. includes specific time allotments to the topics to be taught
    B. reflects the needs, interests, and abilities of the children
    C. provides sufficient time for all subject areas
    D. is flexible to allow for unexpected occurrences

13. Of the following classroom practices, the one which is generally UNDESIRABLE is:

    A. Whenever possible, classroom bulletin boards and charts should be placed at children's eye level.
    B. Windows in the classroom should be covered with crepe paper to make the room attractive
    C. Classroom "centers of interest" should vary from grade to grade in accordance with children's learning needs
    D. A room indicator card should be used to indicate the whereabouts of the class when it is not in the classroom

14. The MOST effective method of helping children to develop the concept of cooperation is to provide

    A. opportunities for listening to stories about children cooperating with each other
    B. speakers to tell about how they cooperated with people of various ethnic groups
    C. audio-visual materials which illustrate the concept of cooperation among ethnic groups
    D. many experiences that will involve them in cooperating with children of different ethnic groups

15. The LEAST effective strategy in stimulating children to express themselves orally in social studies lessons would be for the teacher to

    A. direct questions to specific children and get a response
    B. encourage children to talk with classmates and to give guidance when needed
    C. accept contributions from all the children
    D. help shy children express their ideas

16. Of the following statements regarding pupil discussion, the LEAST valid is:

    A. Use of the amenities helps to move a discussion forward
    B. Discussion of a topic or problem leads to a solution or an agreement
    C. A discussion period allows for an honest interchange of comments among pupils
    D. Discussion by pupils is more or less organized talking directed to a matter of common concern

17. Of the following, the MOST valid reason for using mimeographed sheets for homework assignments for pupils is that

    A. the chance of pupil error in copying the assignment from the blackboard is reduced
    B. they make possible more interesting, varied assignments
    C. if a pupil is absent, there is no problem about getting the assignment
    D. it saves the teacher a good deal of time

18. The FIRST and MOST important step in planning a test is to

    A. decide what kinds of questions are to be used
    B. define the objectives of instruction
    C. determine how much time is to be allocated for testing
    D. determine the ability levels of the students

19. If, as the lesson progresses, the teacher feels that he will NOT be able to cover all of the content included in his lesson plan, he should

    A. eliminate a final summary
    B. halt discussion and write the important notes on the blackboard
    C. conclude the lesson on the following day
    D. discontinue questioning and complete the lesson by lecturing

19.____

20. The MAJOR difference between the developmental lesson and the unit organization is that the unit plan

    A. usually lasts from one week to two months
    B. falls entirely within one subject field
    C. is motivated by some item of current events and is introduced by the teacher
    D. is logically organized around a small subdivision of subject matter

20.____

21. During a lesson, a student who is not paying attention does not hear the teacher's question. The BEST procedure for the teacher to follow is to

    A. repeat the question for the student
    B. have another student repeat the question
    C. elicit the answer from another student
    D. reprimand the student and repeat the question

21.____

22. Good class discussion is LEAST encouraged if

    A. it is guided by questions presented by the teacher
    B. a give-and-take procedure is employed in evaluating the points introduced by the pupils
    C. the slower as well as the better student presents his idea even if it may be of little value
    D. the teacher at the start of the discussion presents his point of view

22.____

23. If a student's answer to a question is so important that it calls for further stress, it is POOR teaching for the teacher to

    A. ask various members in the class to comment on the answer
    B. repeat it for its proper emphasis
    C. follow it with subsidiary queries
    D. use this answer as the basis for his next question

23.____

24. The MOST worthwhile technique for the teacher to check on whether and how well homework assignments are being done is to

    A. collect the assignments daily and return them the next day
    B. walk around the room and examine each student's homework
    C. have appropriate answers read aloud
    D. have the first student in each row examine the assignments

24.____

25. The BEST procedure is to have the aim of a lesson

    A. stated clearly by the teacher at the outset of the lesson
    B. contain more than is achievable during the lesson

25.____

C. erased from the board after it has been accepted and understood by the class
D. grow out of the motivation

26. Of the following, the MOST appropriate summary for a lesson is the one in which the

    A. teacher briefly reviews the highlights of the lesson
    B. students briefly review the highlights of the lesson
    C. students apply to a situation the information learned in the lesson
    D. teacher quizzes the students at the end of the lesson on the information taught in the lesson

27. For an effective final summary, the teacher should

    A. have the pupils repeat the facts learned during the lesson
    B. point out the significant facts himself
    C. determine a summary question as the lesson progresses, rather than in advance of the lesson
    D. seek a recapitulation of the material presented during the lesson

28. In teaching, rapid questioning BEST serves the purpose of

    A. recalling essential facts learned earlier
    B. developing judgment
    C. evaluating viewpoints
    D. recalling concrete experiences

29. An organized discussion of a definite problem by a selected group of pupils in a class is called a

    A. forum               B. symposium
    C. sociodrama          D. debate

30. The BEST method of evaluating the affective outcomes of education is to utilize

    A. anecdotal records kept by pupils
    B. frequent short unannounced quizzes
    C. reports to the class by pupils
    D. standardized tests with national norms

31. The BEST approach for the teacher to use in an effort to enhance pupil participation and the quality of discussion is to

    A. allow volunteers to carry the discussion
    B. restrict the slow or shy pupil who may stall the discussion
    C. discourage the evaluation of student responses
    D. provide an answer himself rather than continually rephrase a question

32. All of the following are examples of behavioral objectives EXCEPT:

    A. "The student can list six links of the infectious disease process."
    B. "Under supervision, the student can safely apply a triangular bandage."
    C. "The student chooses food in the cafeteria that comprises a well-balanced diet."
    D. "The student knows that communicable diseases are caused by microorganisms."

33. An auto-instructional approach to teaching relying on the psychological principles of reinforcement and associative learning is called

   A. programmed instruction
   B. problem solving
   C. socio-dramatization
   D. role playing

34. If a student's answer to a key question posed by the teacher is correct but ungrammatically expressed, of the following, it is WISEST for the teacher to

   A. interrupt the pupil's answer in order to correct the error
   B. ignore the error since the content of the answer is more important
   C. accept it and have the answer rephrased by another student
   D. ask the class what was wrong with the answer

35. In the use of a blackboard, all of the following are desirable practices EXCEPT the one in which the teacher

   A. provides sketches large enough so that they are visible to all pupils in the room
   B. places complex drawings on the blackboard in advance of the lesson to aid in pupils' understanding
   C. keeps all information on the blackboard to assist in the final summarization of the lesson
   D. stands to one side as he sketches a diagram or writes information

36. Of the following, the MOST desirable use of questioning during a lesson is the one which

   A. provides discovery of pupils' inadequate preparation of homework
   B. allows for the learning of the answers the teacher considers important enough to be remembered
   C. checks on pupil inattention during the development of the lesson
   D. focuses pupil attention on important aspects of the topic

37. During a lesson, it is LEAST advisable to use audio-visual material

   A. when a new unit of work is being introduced
   B. during the body of the lesson in which these materials are the basis for the lesson
   C. as a means of summarizing the lesson
   D. as the means of encouraging spontaneous oral student reactions

38. In the planning of developmental lessons, there should be great *similarity* of the

   A. aim and motivation
   B. motivation and medial summary
   C. aim and summary
   D. pivotal questions and summary

39. Note-taking by pupils should be

   A. eliminated since it detracts from the pupils' ability to listen attentively
   B. limited to the recording of the essentials presented during the lesson
   C. used by the teacher as a means of measuring the extent to which a pupil uses his notebook
   D. concerned with the copying of all notes from the blackboard which were presented during the lesson

40. In order to determine if a test question has the ability to discriminate between better and poorer students, the teacher should

    A. compare the results of the better students
    B. compare the results of the poorer students
    C. perform an item analysis
    D. perform a validity and reliability analysis

41. The BEST method of appraising the understandings of students with language difficulties is the use of _____ tests.

    A. essay
    B. oral
    C. objective
    D. standardized achievement

42. If a teacher wanted to elicit from students spontaneous responses regarding any topic, the method she would have the MOST success with is called

    A. role playing
    B. problem solving
    C. brainstorming
    D. self-appraisal

43. The MAIN purpose of a pivotal question is to

    A. direct thought from one aspect of a topic to another aspect of the same topic
    B. have students recall facts related to the topic being discussed
    C. drill students in specific knowledge previously learned
    D. encourage students to come up with a variety of answers

44. In providing for individual differences, of the following, the one that represents the MOST advisable plan for the teacher to adopt is to

    A. allow each child in the class complete freedom of choice in pursuing his projects
    B. have each student apprised of his specific weakness and to work toward correcting it
    C. arrange the students into small groups and plan his work so that the needs of each group are provided for
    D. provide short, frequent tests to determine variations in individual differences and to provide drill to reduce the variations

45. In dealing with slow learners in a heterogeneous class, the teacher should

    A. exempt them from any special reports
    B. spread them throughout the classroom
    C. call upon them only if they volunteer
    D. require them to do the exact same homework assignments as others in the class

46. Of the following, the one which is a disadvantage of grouping bright students together is that

    A. the standard high school curriculum will be covered too quickly
    B. in being with other bright students, these talented pupils become too humble
    C. the teachers with special talents have to be assigned to the bright group at the expense of the rest of the students
    D. it tends to deprive them of leadership opportunities

47. If a class as a whole does very poorly on a full-period unit test, the MOST effective of the following procedures is to

    A. return the papers and warn the pupils they must improve
    B. give another test on the same unit after clarifying the main concepts with which the students had had difficulty and providing remedial instruction
    C. go over the test and then have each pupil bring in two copies of the correct solution of every problem he failed to work correctly
    D. discard the test papers and proceed to the next topic, resolving to deal with it more effectively

47.___

48. Of the following, the one which is usually the LEAST important purpose for giving a quiz is that it

    A. is often part of the learning process
    B. often provides a basis for remedial work
    C. gives an opportunity for additional review and drill
    D. provides objective evidence on which to base marks

48.___

49. Which one of the following principles of learning is the LEAST acceptable?

    A. Concepts and processes should be developed from concrete and familiar situations in the life of the pupil.
    B. The pupils should always understand the reason for a process.
    C. Drill may occasionally be conducted effectively in preparation for understanding.
    D. When a rule is developed, it should be, as far as possible, the pupil's own generalization on the way he solves a problem.

49.___

50. Of the following, the LEAST desirable function of a school club is to

    A. promote interest in a subject and develop a broader understanding of its nature
    B. select bright pupils for a subject team, thus providing opportunities to coach them
    C. discuss with interested students the many applications of the subject
    D. foster special interests and talents along subject lines

50.___

## KEY (CORRECT ANSWERS)

| | | | | |
|---|---|---|---|---|
| 1. B | 11. D | 21. A | 31. A | 41. B |
| 2. D | 12. C | 22. D | 32. D | 42. C |
| 3. C | 13. B | 23. A | 33. A | 43. A |
| 4. D | 14. D | 24. A | 34. B | 44. A |
| 5. A | 15. A | 25. A | 35. D | 45. C |
| 6. A | 16. B | 26. C | 36. D | 46. D |
| 7. A | 17. A | 27. C | 37. D | 47. B |
| 8. A | 18. D | 28. A | 38. C | 48. D |
| 9. A | 19. C | 29. A | 39. B | 49. C |
| 10. D | 20. D | 30. C | 40. D | 50. B |

# TEST 2

DIRECTIONS: Each question or incomplete statement is followed by several suggested answers or completions. Select the one that BEST answers the question or completes the statement. *PRINT THE LETTER OF THE CORRECT ANSWER IN THE SPACE AT THE RIGHT.*

1. Which one of the following questions asked by a teacher is MOST acceptable?   1.____

   A. "The answer to question 5 is what?"
   B. "Mary, is her answer to question 5 right?"
   C. "What is your answer to question 5, George?"
   D. "Class, tell George the answer to question 5!"

2. The technique of using a team teaching design which includes a master teacher, regular teachers and teacher-aides is based MOST directly upon which one of the following concepts?   2.____

   A. Teachers who have served faithfully deserve master teacher status.
   B. Teaching is a complex art requiring different levels of competence and training.
   C. The conservation of public funds is a moral obligation.
   D. Teacher-aides are often more knowledgeable and skillful than teachers.

3. In conducting a developmental lesson, the usually MOST desirable way, among the following, of responding to a student's correct answer to your question is to   3.____

   A. enter a grade in your record book
   B. call on another pupil to answer the same question
   C. follow up with another question
   D. elaborate on the pupil's answer

4. Which one of the following procedures is MOST acceptable to use in class when several pupils make flagrant errors in grammar and usage?   4.____

   A. Correct the students unobtrusively and proceed with your lesson.
   B. Take a few minutes to explain since every teacher is a teacher of English.
   C. Ignore the errors since such deviations are time-consuming.
   D. Write a note to each pupil's English teacher to inform him of the errors.

5. A technique which permits students to talk about their own impressions, opinions, and feelings is called   5.____

   A. a learning activities packet
   B. values clarification
   C. team teaching
   D. individualized instruction

6. Good questioning technique involves all of the following objectives EXCEPT the one in which questions   6.____

   A. are multiple in type in order to satisfy the varying abilities of the pupils in the class
   B. are limited to one or two points in the chain of reasoning

C. follow a predetermined order which develops the train of thought in logical sequence
D. place the burden of thinking upon the student

7. The MOST desirable type of classroom discipline is BEST attained through which one of the following practices?

    A. encouraging traits of self-discipline
    B. including class behavior in the final rating
    C. establishing the idea that rules and regulations will be strictly enforced
    D. anticipating difficulty and sending the first few minor cases of breach of discipline to the chairman or dean

8. If you find a student in one of your classes doing very poorly despite an obviously high potential, the MOST desirable procedure among the following to take is to

    A. refer the student to the guidance counselor
    B. ask the student to bring his parents to school to see you
    C. write a letter to his parents asking them to come to school to see you
    D. interview the student yourself before making any referrals or calling his parents

9. The procedure of requiring students to stand and face the class, when responding, is

    A. advisable because it discourages calling out of answers
    B. inadvisable because it creates an ordeal for the shy student
    C. advisable because it increases audibility of answers
    D. inadvisable because a recalcitrant student would dispute the rule

10. Of the following, the BEST procedure for obtaining the aim of a specific lesson is

    A. for the teacher to state the aim of the lesson and write it on the blackboard so that all will be sure to have it
    B. to elicit the aim from the class and have it written on the board
    C. for the teacher to dictate the aim of the lesson so that all students can get it in their notebooks
    D. to give the aim the previous day so that the students can prepare for the lesson

11. To obtain better results, when a problem has arisen, a teacher should

    A. ignore the problem and not become picayune over every little detail
    B. reprimand the group, knowing that their pride will cause them to work harder
    C. reprimand specific students who have caused the problem in class
    D. learn the positive effects of praise and optimism on his students

12. One method of creating an atmosphere for successful learning is to

    A. compare students with one another
    B. indiscriminately criticize students' abilities
    C. treat students with respect
    D. single out students who are not performing up to standards set by class

13. The prescribed procedure for recording the attendance in the official class is that it     13._____

    A. may be recorded in the roll book by a reliable pupil, with the clear understanding that the teacher assume full responsibility for the accuracy of the report
    B. may be recorded in the roll book by a pupil, provided the teacher checks daily
    C. must be recorded in the roll book by the teacher daily, since it is a legal document, the accuracy of which is imperative
    D. may be kept on a card and, in a day or so, be recorded in the roll book after errors have been corrected, excuse passes obtained, etc., to avoid having corrections frequently made in the roll book itself

14. Which one of the following would be the LEAST effective procedure for insuring a prompt start of a lesson?     14._____

    A. Give a quiz as the initial step in the lesson.
    B. Assign pupils to blackboard work while others copy the next assignment.
    C. Take attendance and call for attention.
    D. Have pupils copy the new assignment and start on a "warm-up" exercise.

15. During a supervised study period on an assignment, the teacher should NOT     15._____

    A. grade test papers and prepare reports
    B. confer quietly with individual pupils about proper study habits
    C. note the common errors made and the difficulties encountered by several pupils and conduct a quiet discussion with these pupils
    D. note the general quality and quantity of the pupils' work and modify plans for subsequent lessons, if necessary

16. A curriculum guide *usually* contains     16._____

    A. specific techniques which the teacher must follow
    B. a file of tests that the teacher can duplicate
    C. a list of cultural and linguistic items which should be covered
    D. the daily lesson plans for the topics to be taught at each level

17. A student should be removed from class     17._____

    A. if he habitually fails to hand in completed assignments
    B. when the positive benefits to the student are outweighed by his negative influence on the group
    C. if he continually falls asleep in class
    D. if he comes late constantly and wears his hat during class

18. A KEY element in developing classroom discipline is     18._____

    A. the socio-economic background of the students
    B. behavior modification
    C. a big, husky male teacher
    D. a strong administration

19. Teachers who assign reference tasks must be sure that children are capable of performing them. Of the following, the task that is LEAST significant is

    A. the assignment should consist of finding answers to fairly specific questions
    B. children should know how to locate printed information in reference books
    C. children are to know that they are to copy word-for-word from the reference book
    D. the information should be available and locatable in the classroom or the school library

20. All of the following are criteria for worth-while homework assignments EXCEPT:

    A. All homework assignments should be written assignments
    B. Homework assignments should serve a valid educational purpose
    C. They should extend the pupil's fund of information or give practice that he needs
    D. Homework assignments should be specific and completely understood

21. The LEAST effective method for dealing with discipline problems in the classroom is to

    A. keep students busy with appropriate assignments
    B. single out difficult children for reprimand before the whole class
    C. make sure children understand what is expected of them
    D. keep expectations within the ability level of children

22. Which one of the following types of learning is stressed in the gestalt psychologists' explanation of how the individual learns?

    A. Classical conditioning        B. Instrumental learning
    C. Perceptual learning           D. Programmed learning

23. The concept that one can train school children to be neat in their appearance and in the care of their belongings by teaching them to be neat in their arithmetic and spelling papers

    A. is a characteristic tenet of the advocates of behavioristic psychology
    B. has been proved by recent experimental studies
    C. has been virtually abandoned by educators today
    D. is of central importance in the development of programs of "life adjustment education"

24. Of the following, the MOST important purpose served by teaching machines is

    A. updating curriculum material presented to the children
    B. eliminating the need for drill work
    C. providing the learner with continuous knowledge of results
    D. teaching the learner systematic study technique

25. Of the following, which one constitutes the GREATEST stumbling block faced by the teacher in helping a pupil learn how to study effectively?

    A. Identifying good methods of study
    B. Teaching pupils how to organize a study routine
    C. Developing motivation to study
    D. Teaching pupils how to pace themselves

26. If the goal of a composition is self-expression, the teacher should base the grade *primarily* on

    A. content and secondarily on form
    B. content and secondarily on appearance
    C. form and secondarily on content
    D. appearance and secondarily on content

27. A printed statement which describes a desired performance by a student is called a

    A. student program
    B. lesson contract
    C. study module
    D. behavioral objective

28. One of the teacher's MOST important tasks is to

    A. provide a variety of purposeful listening activities
    B. repeat students' questions and answers
    C. remain totally silent to students' utterances
    D. give detailed instructions

29. Maximizing class time and maintaining discipline are two categories of

    A. lesson planning
    B. reading exercises
    C. classroom management
    D. group work

30. The BEST way to make classroom dialogue more meaningful to the student is to

    A. personalize questions
    B. use the same techniques consistently
    C. call on students who know the answers
    D. let the student read out of the book

31. Of the following, the LEAST effective method for obtaining pupil participation is to

    A. give a warm-up drill to the entire class
    B. group the class and give different assignments to each group
    C. have pupils answer in concert
    D. use experiences of pupils in the lesson development

32. A test which is too difficult will USUALLY yield scores that fall into a

    A. bell-shaped distribution
    B. negatively skewed distribution
    C. positively skewed distribution
    D. bimodal distribution

33. The MOST desirable routine procedure for going over homework is to

    A. compare answers orally with the class
    B. have students put their work on the board and explain it to the rest of the class
    C. have the teacher do each example together with the class
    D. collect it and mark it outside of class, returning it within a week

34. Of the following characteristics of a good lesson plan, the one which applies LEAST is that it

    A. forms part of a larger unit
    B. helps give direction to the lesson
    C. be adhered to even if vital side issues appear
    D. focuses on a meaningful problem

35. Which one of the following statements concerning the aim of a lesson is MOST valid?

    A. The teacher should write the aim on the blackboard at the beginning of each lesson.
    B. The aim should be an outgrowth of and developed from the motivation.
    C. Each child should write the aim of each lesson in his notebook each day.
    D. The teacher should announce the aim of the lesson to the class at the beginning of each period.

36. If a class you inherit from another teacher is poorly motivated and many of the students talk to one another during lessons, you should NOT

    A. teach carefully planned lessons daily for those who listen and try to ignore the others
    B. look up records of each member of the class and consult the guidance counselor where appropriate
    C. plan lessons in which students change activity every 15 minutes from written work to oral work to reading, etc.
    D. rearrange the seating so that groups who talk to one another are separated as far as possible

37. Among the following, the MOST obvious fact that faces the teacher of a ninth grade class is that

    A. the future doctors, chemists, engineers, and nurses can be accurately identified
    B. the boys are generally more talented in science and math than are the girls
    C. the girls are generally more mature than the boys
    D. the girls prefer the biological aspects of science, while the boys prefer the physical aspects of science and mathematics

38. Which one of the following methods for getting a lesson started promptly is LEAST sound pedagogically?

    A. Have a challenging motivating question on the blackboard at the beginning of the period.
    B. Stand near the door with the marking book and give a demerit to any student who does not sit down and take out his work at once.
    C. Give a quiz on the previous lesson at the beginning of the period.
    D. Stand quietly in front of the room and wait for attention.

39. Of the following, experience with various kinds of tests and measurements utilized for predicting academic success of pupils in advanced high school courses and honor classes in a given subject has shown that

    A. an aptitude test is the most satisfactory single instrument
    B. previous achievement represented by pupil's grades in that subject is best

C. all other factors should be subordinated to the I.Q.
D. the child's motivation is the paramount factor

40. It has been found that "learning by wholes," i.e., being challenged by a total situation, is usually BEST achieved by which one of the following groups?  40.____

   A. Dull-normal pupils
   B. Girls
   C. Pupils whose attention span is small
   D. The brighter pupils

41. MOST psychologists would agree that knowledge of results facilitates learning because it  41.____

   A. makes the learner more cautious
   B. leads to correction of erroneous responses
   C. stresses competition within a peer group
   D. provides the learner with social recognition when results are good

42. Of the following, the factor that has the GREATEST effect in contributing to the quality of pupil learning in the classroom is the  42.____

   A. personality of the teacher
   B. structure of the group
   C. characteristics of the learner
   D. physical aspects of the setting in which learning takes place

43. Of the following, research in the field of learning has MOST closely established the efficacy of  43.____

   A. whole rather than part learning
   B. reward rather than punishment as a stimulus for learning
   C. distributed rather than massed practice
   D. the Law of Exercised advanced by Thorndike

44. Of the following, it is MOST essential that an anecdotal record include  44.____

   A. verbatim quotations by witnesses
   B. a thoughtful interpretation of the child's behavior
   C. an objective description of what the child said and did
   D. a daily log of the problems the child presents

45. Which one of the following is the MOST desirable way of economizing on time during a subject-class period?  45.____

   A. Review the homework only occasionally.
   B. Establish definite routines for the pupils.
   C. Use the blackboard sparingly.
   D. Discourage the asking of questions by students.

46. If, soon after the start of a new term, a pupil in one of your academic classes should refuse to do the class work, which one of the following procedures would, as a general rule, be the BEST one to follow in such a case?

    A. Send the pupil to your chairman immediately.
    B. Assert your authority at once and let him know who is "boss".
    C. Speak to him after class to ascertain the cause of his behavior.
    D. Ignore the pupil but give him a failing mark at the end of the term.

47. Of the following possible criteria for evaluating the success of the teaching of reluctant learners in "second track" courses, the LEAST significant is

    A. achievement on standardized tests
    B. improvement in social behavior
    C. improvement in work habits
    D. improvement over past performance

48. Which one of the following statements about lesson plans is pedagogically sound?

    A. They should be made up at least a month in advance and adhered to strictly so that nothing is neglected.
    B. They are not needed by the experienced teacher.
    C. They should be made up week by week, according to the special needs of each class, and be used flexibly.
    D. They need not include pivotal questions.

49. The PRIMARY aim of assigning homework should generally be to

    A. review for class and term tests
    B. drill
    C. develop habits of working hard
    D. instill concepts

50. The daily homework assignment should USUALLY

    A. not include exercises on the new work if the class understands it
    B. have part devoted to review and part based on the new lesson
    C. consist, at least in part, of reading ahead in the new work to be taught
    D. be patterned after Regents-type questions

## KEY (CORRECT ANSWERS)

| | | | | |
|---|---|---|---|---|
| 1. C | 11. C | 21. B | 31. C | 41. B |
| 2. B | 12. C | 22. C | 32. C | 42. C |
| 3. C | 13. C | 23. C | 33. B | 43. C |
| 4. A | 14. C | 24. C | 34. C | 44. C |
| 5. B | 15. A | 25. C | 35. B | 45. B |
| 6. A | 16. C | 26. A | 36. A | 46. C |
| 7. A | 17. B | 27. D | 37. C | 47. A |
| 8. D | 18. A | 28. A | 38. B | 48. C |
| 9. C | 19. C | 29. C | 39. B | 49. D |
| 10. B | 20. A | 30. A | 40. D | 50. B |

# EXAMINATION SECTION
# TEST 1

DIRECTIONS: Each question or incomplete statement is followed by several suggested answers or completions. Select the one that BEST answers the question or completes the statement. *PRINT THE LETTER OF THE CORRECT ANSWER IN THE SPACE AT THE RIGHT.*

1. The factors in the presentation to which the teacher should give the GREATEST weight are
   A. stage presence, style, and personal appearance
   B. audibility, dramatic expression, and the progress of the student
   C. selection of the tourist attraction, number of points made, and number of errors in French
   D. level of memorization, quality of the written notes, and willingness to stand in front of the room

   1.____

2. How can students BEST be encouraged to listed to classmates as they make their presentations?
   A. Have the creators of the dialogue write key questions on the board for classmates to answer.
   B. Indicate that you will lower the grade of anyone who cannot behave courteously.
   C. Announce that you will ask questions about the attraction based on the previous lessons.
   D. Indicate that you will be in back of the room watching the audience.

   2.____

3. A slowing of the pace of a lesson is in indication that the
   A. students have not had ample time to assimilate the new material
   B. students are bored and are reticent to participate
   C. energy level of the teacher has decreased
   D. teacher has exerted pressure on the students to respond quickly

   3.____

4. Discipline problems can BEST be minimized and/or avoided if the teacher
   A. engages the students in a lot of busy work
   B. plans effectively and provides variety in each lesson
   C. maintains high expectations for all students
   D. penalizes the entire class for the infraction of one

   4.____

5. When teaching a new topic, the teacher should
   A. make sure that all homework difficulties have been corrected before teaching the new material
   B. allow sufficient time for a full presentation of the new material
   C. teach the new material before any discussion of the homework
   D. warn pupils that they will be tested on the new material the next day

   5.____

6. In a comparison of the developmental and lecture method, which one of the following statements is MOST NEARLY CORRECT?
   A. In the lecture method, the teacher readily checks the progress of learning.
   B. There is greater pupil participation in the developmental method.
   C. Greater pupil attention is insured in the lecture method.
   D. There is less need for review at the beginning of a developmental lesson.

6._____

7. When classroom teachers attempt to deal with children's emotional difficulties which are at the basis of much serious misconduct, they are inclined to
   A. plan treatment programs which cover too long a period of time
   B. stress the removal of the cause rather than the elimination of annoying symptoms
   C. deal with immediate rather than basic causes of misconduct
   D. spend too much time assembling unnecessary data before they initiate their treatment program

7._____

8. In teaching that 12 inches equal 1 foot, 3 feet a yard, and 36 inches a yard, a teacher is MOST justified in
   A. providing experience for discovering these facts before helping the children to relate one fact to another
   B. having the children learn the three facts at one time in order to have them see the relationship of one fact to another
   C. not aiming at complete mastery of these facts since they are readily available, when needed, in reference books accessible to children and adults
   D. having the children first memorize the facts and then give them problems to solve in which the facts are applied

8._____

9. If a student in one of your subject classes has not done any homework for two weeks, which one of the following would be the BEST procedure to follow as an initial measure?
   A. Send him to your chairman with a note explaining the situation.
   B. Keep him after school while he makes up the homework.
   C. Discuss with him privately the reasons for his failure to do the homework.
   D. Give him a failing rating on the first report, regardless of his test average.

9._____

10. In seating your classes, it is usually WISEST to do which one of the following?
    A. Rearrange their seats according to marks on tests.
    B. Seat them so that the better students can assist poorer students easily.
    C. Seat them in strict alphabetical order.
    D. Let them sit wherever they wish.

10._____

11. Which one of the following is LEAST likely to succeed in sustaining the attention of slow learners?
    A. A 30-minute film
    B. A 30-minute lecture
    C. A change in activity every 10 minutes
    D. A 20-minute laboratory exercise

11._____

12. That "practice makes perfect" is usually MORE acceptable for  12.____
    A. slow learners than it is for rapid learners
    B. average learners than it is for slow learners
    C. rapid learners than it is for slow learners
    D. superior students than it is for average learners

13. Through which one of the following types of lessons will a teacher be MOST  13.____
    likely to succeed in helping children become able to learn by themselves?
    A. Supervised study           B. Lecture demonstration
    C. Note-giving                D. Laboratory demonstration

14. Of the following, which man has written a series of books on American  14.____
    education?
    A. Jansen      B. Pauling      C. Conant      D. Acheson

15. In connection with teaching a technical term, it is usually BEST to  15.____
    A. develop the concept before giving the term its technical name
    B. introduce the technical term and then develop the concept
    C. give the technical term and define it without follow-up discussion
    D. give the technical term, define it, and then explain the concept to the
       class

16. Of the following possible justifications for surprise quizzes, the BEST one  16.____
    is that
    A. they are periodically necessary to deflate the sense of superiority of the
       students who ordinarily get high marks
    B. it is best to punish a class for poor discipline with these quizzes
    C. they encourage the students to study regularly
    D. they cause the students to have more respect for the teacher

17. Assume that you have just met a class for the first time and that soon after  17.____
    the lesson begins a body makes a loud noise. Usually the BEST of the
    following suggestions for the immediate handling of this situation is to
    A. send him to the dean at once
    B. assign him the task of writing "I must be a gentleman at all times" 200
       times for homework
    C. warn him about the possibility of expulsion from the school
    D. tell him to see you after class; then proceed with the lesson

18. Which one of the following statements concerning the purposes of  18.____
    questioning is MOST reasonable?
    A. Questions should be challenging, arouse attention, stimulate thinking, and
       encourage good expression in the answers given.
    B. Simple, factual questions should be asked often to serve as the teacher's
       best evaluative device.
    C. Questions should be repeated to make sure that every student under-
       stands them.
    D. Multiple questions should be asked occasionally to encourage clear
       thinking in complicated situations

19. Of the following, the one which may BEST be achieved by programmed instruction is
    A. allowing a student to proceed at his own pace
    B. reducing the number of teaching positions
    C. providing study materials for homebound students
    D. providing practice materials for students of low reading ability

19._____

20. Of the following procedures for the handling of the clarification of course objectives and daily aims to the students, the BEST one is for these objectives and aims to be
    A. clearly stated by the teacher
    B. raised by the students, discussed, and accepted by them
    C. written on the blackboard before they are discussed
    D. written on the blackboard after explanation by the teacher and then copied into notebooks by the students

20._____

21. Summaries of learnings elicited during and at the end of a lesson are USUALLY
    A. a waste of time
    B. useful only to slow learners
    C. important in focusing attention on the concepts developed
    D. not as good as summaries dictated by the teacher for copying into pupils' notebooks

21._____

22. When there is some unnecessary commotion in the hallway during a lesson, a teacher should FIRST
    A. shut the door and continue with the lesson
    B. send one of the students to the administrative assistant's office and alert him
    C. step to the door to see what is the cause of the commotion so that he may take appropriate action
    D. send the students involved to the dean's office

22._____

23. Which one of the following statements about lesson plans is LEAST acceptable?
    A. They should be done anew each year even if the same subjects are to be taught.
    B. They continue to become less and less necessary as your years of experience increase.
    C. They should include the actual phraseology of pivotal questions to be asked.
    D. They should be prepared weekly but be flexible enough to permit daily additions and corrections.

23._____

24. Of the following, the BEST approach to use in connection with the reporting of subject-class absentees who are not on the daily official class absentee list is to
    A. be very certain to send in a "cutting" slip for each missing student not on the absentee list, no matter what his record is in the subject-class
    B. select those in whom you have least faith, and send in "cutting" slips for them
    C. wait a week or so before sending in any "cutting" slips and try to use your personal influence on the students as you meet them later
    D. send in one "cutting" slip each day as an example to the others

24.____

25. When the common element in a number of experiences has been recognized and extracted by a student, then the student has MOST likely formed a(n)
    A. percept    B. concept    C. objective    D. hypothesis

25.____

26. Which one of the following is NOT the responsibility of the homeroom teacher?
    A. Encourage average students who are doing poorly in school to drop out of school and go to work.
    B. Discuss with students the possible courses they may request for next term.
    C. Assist students to get help in handling homework difficulties in various subjects.
    D. Encourage students to join school clubs and organizations which will meet their needs.

26.____

27. Of the following, the BEST course of action for a new teacher who is having difficulty in presenting a particular type of lesson to take is to
    A. make an arrangement with an experienced teacher to observe his classes
    B. consult the chairman and request an opportunity for intervisitation
    C. try to adjust without outside help to avoid demonstrating weakness to colleagues
    D. discuss the problem frankly with the class and ask for suggestions from the class

27.____

28. Of the following, the BEST situation for using essay questions is where
    A. it is desired to test the ability of a pupil to organize his answers
    B. the class is made up chiefly of slow pupils
    C. "single shot" questions are needed to complete an examination
    D. it is desired to sample a large area of subject matter

28.____

29. In a lesson in which a new topic is to be taught, which one of the following is the MOST desirable principle to follow?
    A. Make certain that all difficulties encountered by pupils in doing the previous homework assignment have been corrected before beginning the new topic.
    B. Allow sufficient time to include a suitable motivation of the new material, a development, and independent pupil practice.
    C. Introduce the new topic, but require pupils to study the textbook for a complete explanation
    D. Insist that no questions be asked by pupils until the development is completed

30. A test may be said to be reliable when
    A. it consistently measures what it attempts to measure
    B. it adequately deals with the types of educational outcomes to be measured at proper levels of difficulty for pupils
    C. there is a high correlation between test scores and criterion measures
    D. it can be obtained on time from publishers

31. Of the following, the one which does NOT measure the concentration of scores in any set of scores or group of data is the
    A. mode     B. modulus     C. mean     D. median

32. Of the following, the GREATEST advantage of short-answer tests is the
    A. ease with which the test items can be constructed
    B. ease with which such tests can be standardized
    C. wide sampling of the subject matter of the course
    D. ease with which the test results can be interpreted

33. The MOST effective use of the talents and abilities of the able pupils in your subject area would be gained by which one of the following procedures?
    A. Give them extra homework assignments in order to earn better marks.
    B. Give them the responsibility of tutoring disadvantaged pupils.
    C. Give them monitorial duties, such as marking test papers.
    D. Excuse them from classwork which they grasp easily so they do enrichment work in other subject areas.

34. The MAIN advantage of standardized tests is
    A. objectivity
    B. ease of marking for teachers
    C. marks may be compared with other groups
    D. it provides greater motivation for students

35. A percentile score of 55 is
    A. a score equivalent to the arithmetic median of the scores
    B. equaled or exceeded by 45% of the scores in the distribution
    C. equivalent to a score of 55 out of 100
    D. the accepted norm

36. The process of reviewing homework daily is time-consuming. Of the following suggestions made by a group of teachers, which one is MOST sound pedagogically?
    A. Do not go over the homework at all.
    B. Go over in class only the problems with which pupils had trouble.
    C. Collect the homework of only one row at a time and return it corrected the next day.
    D. Collect the homework of the whole class once a week on a specific day.

36.____

37. Which one of the following is the BEST statement about a teacher's technique of questioning?
    A. No question should be so difficult that even the slowest pupil couldn't answer it.
    B. Each lesson should have at least one question which would require the pupils to do critical thinking.
    C. There should be a series of pivotal questions to highlight the chief learning.
    D. Each question should be simple and short.

37.____

38. Of the following, the BEST statement concerning skill in questioning is that
    A. to make sure all students hear, the teacher should often repeat her question
    B. answers should be repeated because some children sit far away from the pupil who is answering
    C. each question should be addressed to a particular pupil by giving his name before asking the question
    D. a question should be addressed to the entire class

38.____

39. When a parent complains to you that you are underrating her son, the BEST procedure, among the following, for you to follow is to
    A. tell the parent that you alone have the moral and legal responsibility for assigning the marks
    B. refer the parent to the principal
    C. agree to raise the grades in the future
    D. explain the grading system and review the pupil's grades with the parent

39.____

40. Which one of the following statements would BEST describe procedures of note-taking in a class of slow learners?
    A. They should have few or no notes at all since they have limited verbal ability.
    B. Mimeographed notes should be given to them since note-taking is frustrating for them.
    C. Notes, of a simple kind, should be developed cooperatively by pupils and teacher.
    D. A few short notes should be copied directly from the textbook to ensure accuracy and reinforce reading skills

40.____

41. In THE AMERICAN HIGH SCHOOL TODAY, James B. Conant proposes that
    A. the four-year high school should be a comprehensive high school
    B. the present curriculum in the fourth year of high school is more appropriate for a "community junior college"
    C. "social living" courses should be added in all high schools to provide better life adjustment in our atomic era
    D. standardized achievement tests, such as State Regents, have outlived their usefulness

41.____

42. The SIMPLEST way, among the following, to exhibit a newspaper clipping to an entire class at one time is to
    A. make a slide for a slide projector
    B. make a highly enlarged Photostat
    C. use the overhead projector
    D. use an opaque projector

42.____

43. Of the following, which combination of activities is LEAST suitable as a homework assignment in preparation for a full-period test?
    A. Study and review all work since (date).
    B. Skim through Chapters 16 and 17. Study your class notes since (date). Review our homework since (date).
    C. Re-read Chapters 16 and 17. Look over the questions at the end of each chapter.
    D. Review all class notes and homework since (date). Do the practice mimeo test distributed today.

43.____

44. In selecting the aim for a developmental lesson, the MOST important among the following considerations is the
    A. content of the previous day's lesson
    B. motivation to be used
    C. decision as to which knowledges, attitudes, or skills should be taught next
    D. content of the syllabus

44.____

45. The validity of intelligence tests as instruments for evaluating native ability has been questioned because these tests tend to
    A. lack reliability, especially for gifted children
    B. lack reliability, especially for pupils of low motor coordination who consequently have a poor sense of spatial relations
    C. place too much emphasis on mathematical and scientific aptitude
    D. have an experiential base which is foreign to culturally different children in poverty areas

45.____

46. Of the following, the MAJOR aim for giving a standardized test to classes        46.____
    at the beginning of a new course is probably to
    A. discover weaknesses of previous teaching
    B. discover interests, aptitudes, and previous learnings in this area
    C. give teachers and supervisors a basis for deciding upon the regrouping of
       classes in terms of ability
    D. arouse pupil curiosity and provide a base for motivation

47. Of the following terms, the one MOST closely associated with the sum total        47.____
    of response patterns and abilities possessed by the learner at any given time is
    A. adaptation           B. readiness
    C. reinforcement        D. response

48. If 48% of your class failed a unit test, the BEST procedure to follow is to        48.____
    A. develop a normal curve on a graph and adjust the grades
    B. ask your chairman to evaluate our test; if he agrees it is fair, re-teach
       parts of the unit, then review and give a new test
    C. chastise the failing pupils sternly and write nots to the parents, if your
       chairman agrees your test is fair
    D. give an "extra credit" test to the failing pupils

49. Of the following reasons for giving homework, the LEAST acceptable reason        49.____
    is that it
    A. extends the learning process beyond the classroom
    B. provides practice in the art of self-study
    C. increases the chances of retentivity
    D. trains the pupils in habits of doing hard work

50. Which one of the following sets of statements BEST explains the occurrence        50.____
    of disciplinary infractions among adolescents in secondary schools?
    A. Adolescents tend to resist authority; they seek the admiration of their
       peers; they are not convinced that poor-self-control is necessarily harmful
       to future success.
    B. Syllabi ae teacher-imposed; rules of conduct in secondary schools are
       unrealistic.
    C. Adolescents undergo raid physical growth; their span of attention is short;
       they are incapable of abstract thoughts.
    D. Adolescence has been extended by modern society; rules of conduct do
       not parallel chronological age; there is a widespread lack of pre-
       vocational meaningful study.

## KEY (CORRECT ANSWERS)

| | | | | |
|---|---|---|---|---|
| 1. B | 11. B | 21. C | 31. B | 41. A |
| 2. A | 12. A | 22. C | 32. C | 42. D |
| 3. A | 13. A | 23. B | 33. B | 43. A |
| 4. B | 14. C | 24. A | 34. C | 44. C |
| 5. B | 15. A | 25. B | 35. B | 45. D |
| 6. B | 16. C | 26. A | 36. B | 46. B |
| 7. C | 17. D | 27. B | 37. C | 47. B |
| 8. A | 18. A | 28. A | 38. D | 48. B |
| 9. C | 19. A | 29. B | 39. D | 49. D |
| 10. B | 20. B | 30. A | 40. C | 50. A |

# TEST 2

DIRECTIONS: Each question or incomplete statement is followed by several suggested answers or completions. Select the one that BEST answers the question or completes the statement. *PRINT THE LETTER OF THE CORRECT ANSWER IN THE SPACE AT THE RIGHT.*

1. Of the following, the generally LEAST acceptable type of short-answer question is
   A. multiple choice
   B. completion
   C. true-false
   D. matching

2. Pupils who seem sensitive, timid, and/or immature usually respond MOST favorably to a teacher's efforts when the teacher uses which one of the following methods?
   A. Reproves them frequently
   B. Punishes even minor infractions
   C. Urges them to enter competitions
   D. Praises even minor progress

3. Which one of the following is the MOST efficient way to distribute duplicated sheets to a class?
   A. The teacher individually hands each pupil a sheet.
   B. A monitor hands each pupil a sheet.
   C. The teacher counts off a set of papers for each column and asks the first pupil in each column to take one and pass the rest back.
   D. A monitor counts off a set of papers for each row and asks the first pupil in each row to take one and pass the rest to the side.

4. Intervisitation among teachers in a department is
   A. *unwise*, because teachers should be creative, not imitative
   B. *wise*, because teachers can gain a great deal from sharing methods and techniques
   C. *unwise*, because teachers do not like to be observed by their colleagues
   D. *wise*, because only the few "master teachers" have ideas which are good enough for the others to use

5. The BEST discipline in a classroom is that which is
   A. instilled by a system of severe penalties
   B. learned by the lecture method
   C. self-imposed by the students
   D. obtained through using interesting visual aids

6. Homework assignments are MOST effective when they are
   A. used to introduce new concepts to a class
   B. used to provide practice for a skill taught that day
   C. given to the class as a whole without differentiation
   D. used in a punitive fashion

7. Of the following devices, the one that is LEAST likely to motivate a skills lesson is
   A. the teacher's announcement that the skill is necessary for success in the course
   B. award of extra credit for quick mastery of the skill
   C. demonstration of pupil weakness and consequent need for the skill
   D. announcement of a test to cover that particular skill

8. In making up a lesson plan, the new teacher should attach MOST significance to
   A. what students are expected to achieve by the end of the lesson
   B. preparation for uniform examinations
   C. textual explanations
   D. medial and final summaries

9. In setting up classroom routines, the teacher is well advised to
   A. be consistent in the application of these routines
   B. allow for variation for individual students
   C. ensure student understanding of the reasons for the routines
   D. consider all of these

10. The MOST effective way to review after a test is to
    A. make a frequency distribution of student errors and reteach areas of demonstrated weakness
    B. review each test question and give students the correct answer
    C. review each test question and have students give the correct answers
    D. ask individual students why they had difficulty with particular questions

11. The BEST way for a teacher to determine how well a lesson has succeeded is to
    A. provide time at the end of the period for immediate application of the new learnings
    B. give a test on the new learnings at the end of the week
    C. review carefully the homework handed in the next day
    D. provide for a brief review of the new learnings at the beginning of the next day's lesson

12. Of the following statements regarding the role of the teacher, the one that does NOT belong is to
    A. develop a consistent and reasonable relationship with students
    B. create a meaningful and motivated instructional program
    C. accept responsibility for helping to maintain school tone
    D. concentrate on covering as much material as possible

13. An effective technique of questioning is to
    A. fix one's vision on a particular student while presenting the stimulus
    B. identify the student to respond before presenting the stimulus
    C. present the stimulus before indicating who is to respond
    D. present the stimulus and permit students to call out their responses

3 (#2)

14. In an oversized class, maximum oral participation is BES achieved through 14.____
    A. students' interaction with their neighbor
    B. choral repetition
    C. the use of a tape as a stimulus
    D. group work

15. Which one of the following procedures would be of MOS value in helping 15.____
    the pupil who has unusually severe difficulty with spelling?
    A. Saying each word distinctly before and after writing it
    B. Tracing the words written in large letters with his finger
    C. Copying a word many times until it becomes automatic
    D. Stressing oral rather than written spelling

16. "Teachers contribute to good discipline by seating children appropriately." 16.____
    In practice, appropriate seating means that pupils
    A. of different ability levels will be intermingled
    B. of different ability levels will be separated into distinct groups
    C. will be seated according to their reading groups
    D. will be allowed to choose their own seats in class

17. In a fire drill, the teacher should 17.____
    A. walk at the front of the line
    B. walk at the rear of the line
    C. walk in the middle of the line, keeping the head and rear of the line under observation
    D. start at the front of the line, and then send the class on ahead as she waits for the last child

18. It is generally accepted that one of the MOST frequent errors made by 18.____
    teachers in teaching reading is
    A. failure to use workbooks to supplement basic readers
    B. failure to have books for recreational reading on more than one level in the classroom
    C. assigning children books that are too difficult for them
    D. over-stress on developing critical thinking in reading activities

19. Current evaluation of curriculum materials indicates that large courses of 19.____
    study are being replaced by
    A. brief pamphlets emphasizing "character education"
    B. joint planning conferences by parents and teachers
    C. reports of pupil-teacher cooperative planning
    D. special bulletins o aspects of teaching and learning

20. In the teaching of arithmetic, it is generally believed that drill should 20.____
    A. either precede or follow understanding
    B. not be used
    C. follow the development of understanding
    D. precede the development of understanding

21. In surveys of the junior high school, the curriculum organization is moving increasingly toward
    A. re-emphasizing the unity of specific subjects
    B. requiring mathematics of all pupils
    C. combining certain subjects with English or the social studies
    D. requiring science as a three-year sequence

22. Which one of the following persons has written important books and articles on the teaching of reading?
    A. E. F. Lindquist
    B. Laura Eads
    C. Raymond B. Cattell
    D. Nila B. Smith

23. Drill in mathematics is MOST effective when the teacher
    A. devotes five or ten minutes of each lesson to drill
    B. plans for specific lessons devoted entirely to drill
    C. plans for drill lessons only when the need arises
    D. provides for drill through homework assignments

24. Pupils should be taught to write mathematical symbols
    A. at the same time as these symbols are presented for their recognition
    B. at the same time as they are introduced to cursive writing
    C. after they understand and can recognize them
    D. at the same time as they are introduced to manuscript writing

25. In selecting poems for presentation to children in the intermediate grades, the teacher should realize that children at this level are MOST likely to enjoy
    A. poems written in blank verse
    B. lyrics
    C. ballads
    D. sonnets

26. Of the following, which type of sound is the EASIEST for beginning readers to discriminate?
    A. Final consonant sounds
    B. Initial consonant sounds
    C. Short vowel sounds
    D. Initial digraph sounds

27. Dave, a sixth-grader who reads on a second-grade level, rejects the books in the classroom that are of appropriate difficulty on the basis that they are "baby stuff." The BEST way of solving this problem is to
    A. delay book reading and confine instruction for a while to word-recognition techniques
    B. use interesting word games such as "Wordo," "Anagrams," "Go Fish," etc. until his confidence in his teacher has increased
    C. use a book that, while difficult for him, is better suited to his interest and enjoyment until his confidence is gained
    D. use an experience-story approach based on Dave's own stories until he is reading on a higher level

28. In the teaching of phonics, instruction should start with
    A. seeing differences in printed symbols
    B. learning the sound of various letters
    C. using picture clues
    D. hearing sounds in spoken words

29. The teacher who strives to be impersonal in her relationship to her pupils is generally LEAST effective with those pupils who
    A. do excellent work
    B. are discouraged
    C. seek to win approbation
    D. are independent and mature

30. The BEST time for systematic teaching of phonics is
    A. at the very beginning of instruction in reading in the first grade
    B. after the child has learned a basic sight vocabulary of more than fifty words
    C. in the fourth grade after the child has learned the alphabet
    D. as soon as the child has attained a mental age of six years

31. Although teacher domination of a classroom is looked upon with disfavor by educational theorists, classes characterized by such firm teacher control generally
    A. spend more time in actual work
    B. afford greater satisfaction to the pupil
    C. increase pupil motivation to obtain high grades
    D. enlist faster pupil cooperation

32. Of the following statements concerning the inclusion of individual and group activities in a playground program, the one MOST sound educationally is:
    A. Group activities should be used exclusively so as to give stress to social values and outcomes
    B. Individual and group activities should be included and equal emphasis given to each
    C. Individual activities should be included only when children request them
    D. Individual activities should be included but greater emphasis should be placed on group activities

33. Of the following procedures, on the part of the teacher, the one which is MOST likely to cause poor discipline is
    A. punishing infractions too severely
    B. threatening disciplinary action and failing to carry out the punishment
    C. failing to identify the true peer leadership among students
    D. being impatient with children

34. In teaching skills in physical education, the BEST order of techniques essential to learning is
    A. participation, demonstration, analysis
    B. demonstration, analysis, participation
    C. analysis, participation, demonstration
    D. discussion, participation, analysis, correction

35. An effective teacher in a playground does all of the following EXCEPT:
    A. Allows for program changes when circumstances make these desirable
    B. Consults parents to learn more about individual children
    C. Comments regularly on the lapses and mistakes that a child makes
    D. Notes the peer judgments of children

36. In the teaching of sports skills, it is recommended that the playground teacher do all of the following EXCEPT
    A. analyze the component parts of the skill clearly
    B. explain the reasons for performing the skill in a specific way
    C. pick a participant at random to demonstrate
    D. provide sufficient opportunity for practicing the skill

37. For the purpose of providing instruction for small groups that require explanation and demonstration, it is generally BEST to arrange the learners in
    A. a circle formation          B. a semi-circle
    C. any random position         D. line formation

38. Of the following, the LEAST important consideration in planning the athletic program of the playground is
    A. the facilities that are available
    B. the age groups of the participants
    C. seasonal interests
    D. the skill and ability of the teacher in the activities selected

39. Of the following responsibilities of the playground teacher, the one which is FIRST in importance is to
    A. provide activities for the participation of the maximum number
    B. emphasize big muscle activity
    C. give individual instruction
    D. introduce new activities

40. Studies comparing the forgetting of completed and incompleted tasks tend to show that
    A. completed tasks tend to be forgotten more rapidly than incompleted ones
    B. incompleted tasks tend to be forgotten more rapidly than completed ones
    C. there is no difference in retention of the two types of tasks
    D. the inconclusive results that have been obtained make it impossible to generalize

41. Of the following, which is generally MOST conducive to the mastery of a skill?
    A. The practice of the skill in a daily routine
    B. Emphasis on speed rather than accuracy in early practice
    C. Overlearning
    D. Lack of emotion and pressure during practice

42. Degree of maturity, amount of previous experience, and motivation are all factors affecting the degree of _____ shown by a learner.
    A. intelligent activity
    B. transfer of skills
    C. readiness
    D. retention

42.____

43. Of the following, which one is of relatively minor effectiveness in determining the amount of transfer of learning from one subject to another?
    A. The degree of relationship between the two subjects involved
    B. The methods used by the teacher to establish a relationship between the subjects involved
    C. The amount of study time put in by the learner on the material
    D. The ability of the learner to make generalizations

43.____

44. Which of the following processes is basic to all learning?
    A. Verbalization
    B. Insight
    C. Trial and error
    D. Discrimination

44.____

45. Modern psychological theory suggests that the success of a classroom learning experience will depend PRIMARILY upon the
    A. motivation of the learner
    B. climate of the classroom
    C. readiness of the learner
    D. personality of the teacher

45.____

46. Research has demonstrated that the MOST efficient way of distributing one's effort in learning
    A. entails scheduling long units of practice with short intervals between units
    B. involves scheduling short units of practice with long intervals between units
    C. calls for units of practice and intervals of approximately equal duration
    D. depends on the material to be learned and the individual learner

46.____

47. As defined by the Gestalt psychologist, "insight" should be looked upon as
    A. a subconscious solution of a problem
    B. a sudden reorganization of experience
    C. a form of creative inspiration
    D. orientation of the learner toward the solution of a problem

47.____

48. The use of rewards and punishments to stimulate learning involves the psychological principle known as the law of
    A. effect
    B. elimination
    C. disinhibition
    D. behavioral facilitation

48.____

49. Which of the following generalizations concerning transfer of training would be accepted by MOST present day psychologists?
    A. Positive transfer is widespread, but it is more specific than general.
    B. Little transfer occurs, but when it does it is more or less general.
    C. There is practically no transfer from school subjects to daily living.
    D. The humanities contribute more to general improvement of thinking than mathematics or science.

49.____

50. Usually, the rate of forgetting material learned in the classroom  50._____
    A. is slow for a short time and then increases rapidly
    B. increases gradually from the time learning occurs
    C. is rapid immediately after learning occurs and then tends to level off
    D. varies depending upon the nature of the material learned

## KEY (CORRECT ANSWERS)

| | | | | |
|---|---|---|---|---|
| 1. C | 11. A | 21. C | 31. A | 41. C |
| 2. D | 12. C | 22. D | 32. D | 42. C |
| 3. D | 13. D | 23. A | 33. B | 43. C |
| 4. B | 14. B | 24. C | 34. B | 44. D |
| 5. C | 15. B | 25. C | 35. C | 45. C |
| 6. B | 16. A | 26. B | 36. C | 46. D |
| 7. C | 17. A | 27. D | 37. B | 47. B |
| 8. A | 18. C | 28. D | 38. D | 48. A |
| 9. D | 19. D | 29. B | 39. A | 49. A |
| 10. A | 20. C | 30. B | 40. A | 50. C |

# GLOSSARY OF LEARNING TERMINOLOGY

# CONTENTS

|  | Page |
|---|---|
| Academic education ...... adult education | 1 |
| adult learner ...... bilingual education | 2 |
| brainstorming ...... community college | 3 |
| community development ...... continuing education | 4 |
| continuing education program ...... credit by examination | 5 |
| curriculum ...... evening college | 6 |
| expansion ...... forum | 7 |
| functional illiteracy ...... homestudy | 8 |
| industrial arts education program ...... involved in the development of the plan | 9 |
| lecture ...... local education agency | 10 |
| manpower ... program | 11 |
| psychometric ....... retraining | 12 |
| self-directed-learning ........ technical education | 13 |
| trainee ....... workshop | 14 |

# GLOSSARY OF LEARNING TERMINOLOGY

**academic education**    The theoretical, the liberal, the speculative, and classical subject matter found to compose the curriculum of the public secondary school. (The Adult Education Act–P.L. 95-561.)

**accountability**    Responsibility for a specified performance, outcome, result.

**administration**    The function provided by management in the planning, organizing, initiating, coordinating, operating, evaluating and revising procedures; or programs directed towards the completion of an assigned task or achievement of a goal.

**adult**    Any human being, past the age of puberty, who has discontinued his full-time attendance in a formal school situation, and functions in one or more adult life roles, viz, spouse, parent, worker, or any human being who has reached the legal and/or socially prescribed age for assumption of adult rights, privileges and responsibilities.

**adult**    Any individual who has attained the age of sixteen. (The Adult Education Act–P.L. 95-561.)

**adult basic education**    Any purposeful effort toward self-development in the basic skills of communication, computation, health, consumer development, and citizenship carried on by an adult who is generally classified as functionally illiterate or undereducated.

**adult basic education**    Adult education for adults whose inability to speak, read, or write the English language constitutes a substantial impairment of their ability to get or retain employment commensurate with their real ability, which is designed to help eliminate such inability and raise the level of education of such individuals with a view to making them less likely to become dependent on others, to improving their ability to benefit from occupational training and otherwise increasing their opportunities for more productive and profitable employment, and to making them better able to meet their adult responsibilities. (The Adult Education Act–P.L 95-561.)

**adult education**    A process by which the instructional needs of an adult, as perceived by themselves or others, are met through organized learning experiences.

**adult education**    Services or instruction below the college level for adults who lack sufficient mastery of basic educational skills to enable them to function effectively in society or who do not have a certificate of graduation from a school providing secondary education and who have not achieved an equivalent level of education, and are not currently required to be enrolled in schools. (The Adult Education Act–P.L. 95-561.)

**adult learner** — An adult who is enrolled in any course of study, whether special or regular, to develop new skills or qualifications, or improve existing skills and qualifications.

**advisory council** — A group of persons created to give advice on a particular project, program or organization.

**agency** — (1) An institution or group, formal or informal in structure, formed and operating to alleviate and to serve specific needs of individuals in a neighborhood, community or city; (2) a group of dedicated persons identified with a specific area of services.

**ancillary services** — The supportive activities and resources necessary for the efficient achievement of the objectives of an organization or institution.

**andragogy** — The art and science of teaching adults and of adult learning in a climate where the adult is given primary consideration: contrasted with pedagogy.

**appraisal** — A general evaluation of an activity, program, experience, or achievement, often semi-intuitive and of limited sophistication.

**apprenticeship** — A period of time during which a person learns a trade, skill, or role by practice and supervision.

**assessment** — The process of measuring change which has been incurred by an educational experience.

**associative learning** — Learning acquired by association of ideas, e.g., in identified relationship such as opposition, sequence, cause and effect.

**attitude change** — Some degree of change in the internalized or personalized feelings one has about persons, places, things, or events. Although the change presents a shift in the individual's position, it may shift in either a negative or a positive direction from the original one.

**audiovisual aids** — A broad range of devices used to enhance and facilitate information transfer, with emphasis on seeing and hearing, and ranging from simple classroom equipment (e.g., blackboard, felt board) to projected slides, maps or diagrams, sound recordings, silent or sound film strips, films, and videotapes.

**bilingual education** — Historically considered to be a pretty pure form of simply teaching the individual to handle two different languages. Current emphasis is often placed on the teaching of English as a Second Language, for both the average foreign student and the culturally deprived.

| | |
|---|---|
| **brainstorming** | An unstructured, almost casual but highly supportive discussion of ideas with emphasis on rapid, free-wheeling production of a variety of inputs, as opposed to carefully considered, practical steps. All participants supposedly have the complete freedom to make suggestions. They should be positively supportive of the atmosphere, and generally quite willing at least to consider any suggestions offered by any member of the group. |
| **career** | One's progress through life; one's advancement or achievement in a particular vocation or profession to which one gives a professional and personal commitment. |
| **career education** | The conscious and structured effort on the part of an individual, either through their own or through beneficiary efforts of institutions, employers and technical and professional societies, to advance their proficiency, peer recognition and public acceptance in terms of occupational aims. |
| **certificate of completion** | A document attesting to the fact that a person has completed a specific set of learning experiences under sufficient supervision to be sure that the awardee did the prescribed work. There may or may not be formal classes, formal reading, or formal examinations. |
| **change agent** | Person, group or thing that effects or seeks to effect changeparticularly an agent for change of social conditions. |
| **citizen population** | The inhabitants of a city, town, state or country who are eligible to vote and participate in the deliberations of governmental processes. |
| **citizenship education** | Teaching people how to become effective citizens. |
| **class** | The basic unit in the organizational structure of most formal learning; generally a group of learners which meets regularly for a fixed term to be instructed in one or more subjects or in an entire curriculum. A recent trend has been toward a more open and flexible grouping of students, based on their own interests or abilities. |
| **clientele** | That specific sub-group of the general population for which an institution, agency, or professional practitioner has a special interest, relationship and/ or reason for being. |
| **clock hour** | A total of sixty minutes of class work of instruction. |
| **communication skills** | The capability for making oneself understood orally or in writing. |
| **community college** | An educational institution above the high-school level offering educational and training opportunities in skills, subject matter and other allied areas. Activities and offerings may be with or without credit, the goal being to offer the people in the community the educational opportunities they lack and desire. |

| | |
|---|---|
| **community development** | Educational efforts with individuals and groups for the purpose of improving the material, social, and aesthetic aspects of the life of the people living in a clearly defined geographical area. |
| **community relations** | The reciprocal pattern of interaction among members of a community that persists over a period of time so that a stable set of social expectations develop. |
| **community school program** | A program in which a public building, including but not limited to a public elementary or secondary school or a community or junior college, is used as a community center operated in conjunction with other groups in the community, community organizations, and local governmental agencies, to provide educational, recreational, cultural, and other related community services for the community that center serves in accordance with the needs, interests, and concerns of that community. (The Adult Education Act–P.L. 95-561.) |
| **community service program** | An educational program, activity, or service including a research program and a university extension or continuing education offering, which is designed to assist in the solution of community problems in rural, urban, or suburban areas, with particular emphasis on urban and suburban problems, where the institution offering such programs, activity, or service determines; (1) that the proposed program, activity, or service is not otherwise available, and (2) that the conduct of the program or performance of the activity or service is consistent with the institution's over-all educational program and is of such a nature as is appropriate to the effective utilization of the institution's special resources and the competencies of its faculty. (The Higher Education Act–P.L. 94-482.) |
| **community student** | An individual who attends a class regularly but who travels a certain distance back and forth to secure the course they desire or need. |
| **competency** | The requisite ability to perform a specific task or qualify for a specific role; a functional qualification as opposed to a credential-based qualification. |
| **conference** | An activity generally involving a large number of individuals sharing a common interest, planned for the dissemination of information to the participants and the collection of feedback from them in limited time. Usually included are expert speakers making single presentations or appearing on panels, alternating with small group discussion among the participants. |
| **consultant** | Resource person available for expert or professional advice in the solution of a problem or achievement of a goal. |
| **continuing education** | Any purposeful effort toward self-development carried on by an individual without direct legal compulsion and without such efforts |

becoming his major field of activity, with emphasis on university or senior college level efforts to provide this education.

**continuing education program** — Postsecondary instruction designed to meet the educational needs and in-terests of adults, including the expansion of available learning opportunities for adults who are not adequately served by currenc educational offerings in their communities. (The Higher Education Act–P.L. 94482.)

**cooperation** — The working together toward a common end in a joint action.

**cooperative education** — The linking of formalized education with the real world in which the learner is permitted the opportunity to apply that which is learned in a formal context to a problematic situation in the real world.

**cooperative extension education** — A unique cooperative venture between federal, State, and county govern- ments, with the State land-grant colleges serving as administrative centers. Heavy emphasis is on agriculture and home economics, but the program has expanded to include health, community development, conservation, and public affairs. It relies mostly on non-classroom methods.

**coordination** — The function of bringing persons, groups, and institutions into unity for a common cause or common action.

**coordinator** — The individual responsible for unifying individuals or groups working for a common cause or action.

**correspondence education** — An educational process designed to transfer a given body of information, skills, or knowledge to learners living at some distance from the teaching institution. Usually, written or printed materials are sent by mail, providing the learner with structured units of information, assigned exercises for practice, and examinations to measure achievement. There is an increased use of a variety of teaching-learning media.

**counseling** — The art of helping an individual to solve a problem adequately through personal interaction.

**course** — A planned sequence of educational activity, leading to the acquisition of a skill or body of knowledge, usually over a predetermined period of time.

**credit by examination** — (1) Credit earned through the applicant's successful completion of a pro- ficiency test in place of performing activities ordinarily associated with formal course work; (2) the process of certifying achievement by systematic observation of desired behavior.

| | |
|---|---|
| curriculum | A planned sequence of several educational activities, leading to the acquisition of specified skills or bodies of knowledge, either in a given period or in a given subject or group of subjects. |
| data | Useful facts or information used in making decisions and drawing conclusions. |
| day care | Provide for the direct care and protection of infants, preschool, and school age children outside of their own homes during a portion of a 24-hour day. (Rules and RegulationsFederal Register, April 3, 1980.) |
| delinquent person | An individual who does not abide by and conform to societal behavioral standards that are acceptable to the majority within their environment. |
| diagnosis | (1) The process or procedure of determining the nature of a problem or disorder; (2) a professional judgment made concerning a problem and possible solutions using tests and other appropriate devices. |
| diploma | A certificate given by a school or educational institution testifying that a student has earned a degree or completed a course of study. A certificate conferring some honor or privilege. |
| disadvantaged person | Given an idealized norm, any person who has not reached that norm because of external forces or conditions can be described as disadvantaged. |
| drop in | An individual who participates or who reestablishes his participation in an educational activity on an informal, irregular basis. |
| dropout | An individual who discontinues a course, program of study, or educational endeavor before completing the scheduled period of the activity. |
| education | Any purposeful effort toward self-development carried on by an individual, or one that is planned to afford man the opportunity to continually structure and restructure his cognitive and affective worlds. |
| enrollee | A person who signs up, enlists, volunteers, registers, or contracts to be a student, participant, learner, subject, or pupil in a course, class, workshop or other learning situation. |
| environment | The conditions–physical, social, cultural, and psychologicalthat act upon and influence the life of an individual, group or community. |
| evaluation | An appraisal of an activity, seeking to measure the extent to which the activity attained the objectives set forth. |
| evening college | The division of an institution offering a program of college-level study in late afternoon or evening intended primarily for adults (but also |

**expansion** An increase in the number of agencies, institutions, and organizations other than local educational agenciesused to provide adult education and support services plus one or both of the following two conditions: an increase in the number of adults least educated and most in need of assistance participating in the adult education program; and/or an increase in the percentage of these adults who met their educational objectives. (Rules and Regulations–Federal Register, April 3, 1980.)

**experiential learning** The active involvement and participation of the learner in a contrived or actual exercise that requires the learner to respond covertly or overtly. The learning activity is planned to provide the learner opportunity to actually experience that which is to be learned.

**extension agent** An individual who represents a college, university, or government agency and demonstrates operational techniques, teaches groups about valuable information, or trains individuals or groups in new skills. Historically, extension agents became best known through their use by the U.S. Department of Agriculture.

**extension education** Education offered outside the formal framework of the regular-university, residential-setting, credit-giving approach. It ordinarily includes such methods as conferences, short courses, institutes, independent study, credit courses offered in off-campus settings or via television or other media.

**facilitator** An individual who, like a catalyst, makes particular action possible by his presence and his know-how.

**family group** Those individuals who by kinship, marriage or other affiliation interact as a primary reference group and consider themselves a household.

**feedback** A process by which useful data on a graduate or an aspect of a program or activity is made available to the individuals responsible for the program activity or process. It is a corrective loop whereby information on a program, product or activity is recycled for program improvement and renewal.

**forum** (1) A single event, or a series of events, usually of brief duration (from an hour to less than one day) and usually open to a broad spectrum of individuals who gather to hear a speaker or speakers on a given topic. Generally, opportunities are provided to ask questions of the speaker, but with no structure for organized discussion or feedback; (2) in the abstract, it is also used to denote an opportunity, intended or not, for people to express their opinions.

| | |
|---|---|
| **functional illiteracy** | A quality attributed to an individual who lacks one, or a combination, of the basic skills necessary to communicate effectively in written or arithmetic forms. |
| **functional literacy** | That amount of ability in reading and writing that will permit the individual to perform duties and assume responsibilities above the minimal level. |
| **general education** | Broad-based education that is aimed at helping persons acquire an understanding and appreciation of their environmentwith emphasis on the past, present and future. |
| **general educational development test** | The GED Test is to provide a valid means of measuring the educational proficiency of these persons in comparison with high school graduates. Through achievement of satisfactory scores on a battery of GED Tests, adults may earn a high school equivalency credential, qualify for admission to college or other training programs, meet educational requirements for employment or promotion, satisfy educational qualifications for induction into the Armed Forces of the United States, and meet education requisites of state and local licensing boards for admission to licensing examinations for those occupations requiring educational competence at grade levels less than high school graduation. Thus, the basic purpose of the GED Tests is to provide a second chance for adults who did not complete their formal secondary schooling. |
| **graduate** | A person who has satisfactorily completed certain prescribed requirements indicating they are ready to proceed to the next step or that he qualifies for a degree or a certain profession, occupation or position. |
| **grant** | (Noun) A formal gift of something (e.g., money, land, or a right), usually executed for a designated purpose. |
| **guidance** | A process of offering information and possible alternatives around the needs of the individual so that he can make his own choices and decisions. |
| **high school completion** | (1) Satisfactory completion of a recognized secondary school curriculum (usually four years) leading to a diploma; (2) any satisfactory combination of day and night center high school courses that fulfills the time/activity requirements set by the state for a four-year high school diploma. |
| **high school equivalency** | The granting of high school completion status by virtue of demonstrated ability, usually by written test, in lieu of fulfillment of regular course requirements. |
| **homestudy** | Courses designed for persons unable to attend a class who can work alone at own speed with a minimum of professional assistance |

to obtain course credits, degrees, or competence in skills. Study is usually done by correspondence with occasional communication face-to-face or through the media.

**industrial arts education programs** — Those education programs (A) which pertain to the body of related subject matter, or related courses, organized for the development of understanding about all aspects of industry and technology, including learning experiences involving activities such as experimenting, designating, constructing, evaluating, and using tools, machines, materials, and processes and (B) which assist individuals in the making of informed and meaningful occupational choices or which prepare them for entry into advanced trade and industrial or technical education programs. (The Vocational Educational Act–P.L. 94-482.)

**inner city resident** — Any person living within a large city (over 100,000) and in that portion of such a city that is very close to the center of the city or is in the older, poorer, more run-down portion of that city. Inner city originally was a geographic reference. Now, however, the term means the slum section, and inner refers to differentiation from the suburbs or better-off sections of the city itself.

**institute** — A series of meetings centering upon a particular subject area or problem, lasting one or more days, which are designed to prepare leaders for selected activities or to assist them in solving particular problems of mutual concern. The term frequently refers to the establishment of a special program for adult education. In this case, the term not only refers to the nature of the program but also includes information establishing the geographical location of the program, the nature of the clientele being served, and the educational technologies which are applied.

**instructor** — The person responsible for organizing the teacher-student materials, equipment, facilities, curriculum and teaching methods necessary to enable the student enrolled to make progress toward the educational goals of both himself and society.

**in-service training** — Various kinds of teaching-learning experiences, at least loosely described and defined, designed to help individuals already engaged in professions, vocations or occupations to perform more effectively that which they are already supposed to be doing reasonably well.

**intern** — A supervised individual who applies a program of study in a real or simulated setting.

**involved in the development of the plan** — The representatives of the various agencies and groups are given an opportunity to actively participate in all stages of formulating the plan. In this way, the regulations assure substantive involvement without prescribing the methods or mechanisms through which diverse involvement is achieved. This allows maximum flexibility to a State educational agency while also assuring that token participation will not qualify a State to receive funds. This should not be interpreted to mean that a State educational agency is prohibited from altering its plan or program in the interest of meeting the educational needs of adults. A State educational agency develops procedures and methods for involving the required agencies and groups that best meet the particular needs, problems, and uniqueness of the respective State. (Rules and Regulations–Federal Register, April 3, 1980.)

**lecture** — A formal, one-way verbal technique of communication in which the speaker conveys information to an audience on a specific subject in which the speaker hopefully possesses some expertise.

**leisure education** — Learning activities designed to develop knowledges, insights, skills, attitudes, values, and interests related to the constructive use of leisure time.

**liberal education** — Education that fosters an awareness and appreciation of the intellectual and aesthetic achievements of civilization, independence of mind, and critical, analytical and creative thought.

**library** — A facility closely related to learning activities of adults, providing a variety of materials—book, non-book, multi-media—easily accessible to the persons for whom it is operated; a facility for assisting in acquiring needed data and information, developing a taste for furthering knowledge, developing/expanding a desire to continue learning.

**lifelong learning** — The process by which an adult continues to acquire, in a conscious manner, formal or informal education throughout their life span, either to maintain and improve vocational viability or for personal development.

**lifelong learning** — Includes, but is not limited to, adult basic education, continuing education, independent study, agricultural education, business education and labor education, occupational education and job training programs, parent education, postsecondary education, preretirement and education for older and retired people, remedial education, special educational programs for groups or for individuals with special needs, and also educational activities designed to upgrade occupational and professional skills, to assist business, public agencies, and other organizations in the use of innovation and research results, and to serve family needs and personal development. (The Higher Education Act–P.L. 94-482.)

**local education agency** — A public board of education or other public authority legally constituted within a State for either administrative control or direction of public elementary or secondary schools in a city, county, township, school district, or other political subdivision of a State, or such combination of school districts or counties as are recognized in a State as an administrative agency for its public elementary or secondary schools, except that, if there is a separate board or other legally constituted local authority having administrative control and direction of adult education in public schools therein, such term means such other board or authority. (The Adult Education Act–P.L. 95-561.)

**manpower** — Human resources available to perform work.

**manpower development** — The process of determining the optimum methods of developing and utilizing the human resources of a nation and/or organization. Includes identifying skills required, education, and development programs.

**mentor** — A coach or tutor: an individual who sponsors, teaches and guides others.

**migrant worker** — An individual that moves from one area to another for seasonal work.

**minority group** — A segment of the population which differs from the majority of the population in terms of ethnic group, religion, race, and/or economy.

**noncredit course** — A series of related educational meetings which are programmed and conducted under the auspices of an educational agency. Courses coming under this definition do not carry credit toward diplomas, certificates, or degrees.

**norm** — (1) A standard of performance; (2) the level of achievement or performance of the model group of a population.

**objective** — Aim or purpose of a course of action.

**organization development** — The improvement of the structure, procedures, relationships, environmen- tal quality, and productivity of a social system through development of increased competencies in its personnel.

**out of school youth** — A school-aged person who has not completed an instructional program and who is not participating in an instructional program.

**paraprofessional** — An intermediate skill level between professional and non-professional within a given occupational category.

**pedagogy** — The Science or profession of teaching; also, the theory or the teaching of how to teach.

**pre-service training** — Training received to prepare one to engage in the successful performance of a job or a task.

**program** — The total set of procedures, methods, strategies, objectives, and arrangements which are provided in order to move a student or group of students through a series of educational activities, all of which are designed to achieve pre-determined instructional objectives.

**psychometric** — Applying mathematical methods in analyzing psychological data; a psychological measure.

**question-and-answer method** — An instructional method providing an exchange between an individual who makes an inquiry and an individual who has the competence to respond.

**reading level** — The level of achievement reached by a reader as assessed by an informal inventory or a standardized test. Three reading levels are often considered: *Frustration level,* when the individual makes so many mistakes that he is uncomfortable; *Instructional level,* one grade placement above frustration level; and *Recreational level,* one grade placement above instructional level.

**registrant** — A person who has registered for a particular educational program, but who may or may not actually participate in the program.

**registration fee** — Charge assessed individuals or their sponsors, singly or in groups, for the right to participate in an educational experience. The fee may be nominal, covering the cost of registering and entering the fact upon a record, or the fee may cover any part of the cost of instruction and individual maintenance, including incidentals (e.g., overhead, use of libraries and computers, parking, meals, lodging).

**rehabilitation** — To restore an object or person to a former condition of useful and meaningful capacity and efficiency.

**reliability** — The extent to which a device will provide the same measurement when it is repeated.

**remedial education** — An adult program designed to raise the level of competence of an individual in basic subject areas to that which he should have reached during the time spent in elementary and secondary education. Level may be interpreted as that required to function adequately in present-day society. Adult Basic Education and High School Equivalency Programs may be considered examples.

**resource person** — An individual whose experience and knowledge are of value in helping to plan, to operate efficiently, and to meet and solve problems.

**retraining** — An educational process whereby selected clientele, who have acquired specific skills that seem outdated, are taught new skills designed to better prepare them for changing economic and social conditions. Retraining frequently involves the changing of attitudes and the acquisition of new knowledge prior to skill acquisition.

| | |
|---|---|
| **self-directed-learning** | A systematic process in which an individual takes responsibility, in collaboration with others, for diagnosing his own learning needs, formulating his learning objectives, planning and engaging in a sequence of learning experiences to achieve these objectives, and evaluating progress toward these objectives. |
| **seminar** | A group of individuals who meet regularly with a leader or teacher to explore and discuss selected problems or topics of mutual interest. The seminar frequently includes discussion of original research. |
| **sequential learning** | A scheme of learning which provides for increasingly more difficult and abstract learning built upon previously acquired knowledge, skills, attitudes, and values, and which is planned to build cumulatively toward desired outcomes. |
| **staff** | Personnel of an organization, from professional to custodial, who have assigned functions to carry out the purposes and objectives of the organization. |
| **state education-agency** | The State board of education or other agency or officer primarily responsible for the State supervision of public elementary and secondary schools; or if there is a separate agency or officer primarily responsible for supervision of adult education in public schools, then such agency or officer may be designated for the purpose of this title by the Governor or by State law. If no agency or officer qualifies under the preceding sentence, such term shall mean an appropriate agency or officer designated for the purposes of this title by the Governor (The Adult Education Act–P.L. 95-561.) |
| **student** | An individual who is participating in an educational program. |
| **supervisor** | An individual who is assigned the responsibility of helping some or all staff members, of reviewing the work of another individual or group, and of rating the service in reference to acceptable standards. |
| **teacher** | One who shares knowledge, insight, sensitivity and skills with persons in a learning situation. |
| **teaching** | Facilitating the exploration of a body of knowledge and/or the development of a skill. |
| **technical education** | (1) The body of knowledge that deals with technology; (2) a situation in which an area of ideas and concepts are related to skills. |

| | |
|---:|:---|
| trainee | A person who is in the process of acquiring a definite and prescribed set of skills and qualifications. |
| training | Learning experience leading to the acquisition of a skill. |
| underemployed person | An individual whose skills/qualifications are greater than those required for the position he presently occupies. |
| unemployed person | (1) Any person who is not working or who is not employed in some income-producing activity; (2) a person who wants to work, and is in the age bracket where it is expected that he or she will be self-supporting, who has a need for income, and is acceptable in the working force, but is not working. |
| unskilled worker | Any employee whose work does not require specialized training or knowledge. Tasks are almost always physical in nature and of a routine character. The primary requirement is the ability to follow simple directions. |
| up-grading | Raising the performance or educational level of individuals or organizations. |
| validity | The extent to which a device measures what it purports to measure. |
| vocational education | Any educational experience that is entered into in order to acquire the skills and knowledge necessary to perform a specified set of job-related goals. |
| vocational-education | Organized educational programs which are directly related to the preparation of individuals for paid or unpaid employment, or for additional preparation for a career requiring other than a baccalaureate or advanced degree.(The Vocational Education Act–P.L. 94-482,) |
| volunteer | An individual who performs a task without expecting some form of compensation for the service, time, or function performed. |
| workshop | A teaching-learning experience in which a group of people come together for the specific purpose of both listening and doing. Emphasis is usually on active involvement by participants, e.g., discussion and working toward the solution of a problem-oriented situation. Frequently the participants have similar backgrounds and common interests. |

www.ingramcontent.com/pod-product-compliance
Lightning Source LLC
Chambersburg PA
44116CB00014B/2487